The Gratitude Effect

The Gratitude Effect

Dr. John F. Demartini

Stonebridge books

First published by BurmanBooks Inc., Toronto, Canada
This edition first published by Stonebridge Books, a division of Jacana Media (Pty) Ltd in 2008

10 Orange Street
Sunnyside
Auckland Park 2092
South Africa
+2711 628 3200
www.jacana.co.za

ISBN 978-1-920292-00-3

Cover design by Jack Steiner Graphic Design
Initial Transcriber/Editor: Natalya Androsova
Set in Sabon 12/16pt
Printed by CTP Book Printers
Job No. 000628

See a complete list of Jacana titles at www.jacana.co.za

Titles also by Dr John F. Demartini

Count Your Blessings – The Healing Power of Gratitude and Love

The Breakthrough Experience – A Revolutionary New Approach to Personal Transformation

How to Make One Hell of a Profit and Still get to Heaven

Table of Contents

The Gratitude Effect is dedicated to those individuals who would love to forever expand their physical capacity, mental awareness and spiritual potential – to those who inwardly know there is something magnificent within them and within the universe that surrounds them – to those who sense a hidden order in their apparent daily chaos.

CHAPTER 1

What is the Gratitude Effect?

Gratitude is not only the greatest of virtues,
but the parent of all the others.
– *CICERO*

I was born on Thanksgiving Day – my mother, it would seem, wanted me to be a grateful person. She destined me to involve myself with what I would call "the Gratitude Effect." One day, when I was about four years old, she sat on my bed, leaned over to me and said, "Son, you must always count your blessings because those who count their blessings and are grateful for their life, receive more to be grateful for." I never forgot her inspiring words. Those morsels of wisdom have governed my life ever since. It was also those words that initiated me into – the Gratitude Effect.

I Will be Grateful When There's Something to be Grateful For

We count our miseries carefully,
and accept our blessings without much thought.
– *CHINESE PROVERB*

Any moment of our life that we cannot recall with gratitude is a moment that we have not fully examined. Had we examined that moment, we would have recognized the magnificent hidden order that some philosophers and theologians call the secret workings of the divine master plan. In actuality, not just in our limited sensory reality, there's nothing but love, nothing but a higher, often hidden, order, or conserved and synchronous balance existing throughout all of nature. As Albert Einstein had said: "*Certain it is that a conviction, akin to religious feeling, of the rationality or intelligibility of the world lies behind all scientific work of the higher order. This firm belief, which is bound up with deep feeling, in a superior mind revealing itself in the world of experience, represents my conception of God.*"

I have been blessed to have had the opportunity to travel extensively for many years, and, during my travels, I have asked people from all around the world, "If you had only twenty-four hours to live, what would you do?" And consistently, everyone said, "If I had only twenty-four hours to live, I would say 'thank you' and 'I love you' to those who have most contributed to my life." I also asked people, "How would you prefer to be loved and appreciated?" And all of them, regardless of colour, creed, age, gender, or faith, want to be loved and appreciated for who they actually and authentically are, for their whole true self.

What is there not to love and appreciate? I have been fortunate enough for having had both nature and nurture guide me towards the very mission of honouring this great loving order with humble gratitude. This is one of the reasons for my writing about the *Gratitude Effect*.

If human beings want to be loved and appreciated for who they truly are then love and appreciation must be the very essence of our human existence. So I set out on a quest to discover what this state called gratitude is. And I learnt that gratitude meant thankfulness, appreciation and grace. Gratitude emerges when what we desire and expect matches what actually is, or when our own human will or intention matches what theologians have called the divine will and hidden order. When we have gratitude and humbleness for divinity, we are provided certainty and gratitude for humanity. But when our perceptions and emotions are unbalanced, and we don't recognize the beautiful balance of the divine order, we have our will pushing against divine will, and we become ungrateful for what actually is.

Many people assume that true *gratitude* arises when they perceive their individual values as being supported more than challenged, and when they can easily and superficially count their blessings. These same people may also assume that *ingratitude* arises when they perceive their values as being challenged more than supported, when they can easily count their curses. But this is not the whole picture, for true and deep gratitude, which brings tears of inspiration to our eyes, arises only when we truly awaken to and acknowledge the hidden order and perfect balance residing in our lives and in the entire universe, when both support and challenge and all other complementary opposites are recognized as occurring simultaneously. This is the moment true gratitude spontaneously emerges from within our hearts, and it is the moment we access our most powerful source of love that gives rise to the Gratitude Effect.

There's Something Missing in my Life. How can Gratitude Help Me Find It?

Be thankful. Cultivate an "attitude of gratitude." Thankfulness is much more dependent on attitude than circumstance. When you feel the lack of what you don't have, thank God for what you do have!
– *JIM STEPHENS*

Looking at my own life and lives of people I have had the opportunity to work with, I have noticed that all of us have something we are seeking in life. All of us have a desire to expand our awareness and potential. But because what we perceive through our senses is limited, we can only see, hear, smell, taste, and feel only a minute fraction of what is actually available to us in our infinite existence. In other words, we experience a finite reality compared to the actual infinite. Therefore, there is the actual infinity of divinity that remains hidden, and the real "fininity" of humanity that is revealed. So, because of our endless desires, our life's journey is never quite finished. I call it "infinished".

We are looking at the universe through telescopes and microscopes, but their magnifying capacity has not exceeded a certain level. So, the vastness and the minisculeness of the domains above and below escape us. The universe is infinite, but because of our limited awareness, we can only perceive this tiny domain we call reality. That which is beyond it is always a mystery. That which is within it is already history. Why history? Because it takes a few milliseconds for us to sense something and to register it within our consciousness, so it's always in the past.

Now we have a mystery and a history on our hands – an approximation of the infinite and the realization of the finite. But since we always have something that is unavailable to our immediate sensory awareness, we have this drive for the unknown. I call it a void driving the value to explore and to expand. I've never seen anyone who gets up in the morning and says, "I want to be less spiritually aware, or have less of a mind, and be totally unfulfilled in my career. I want to have less money than I had yesterday, and I want to be able to reduce the number of people in my family. I want to have fewer friends and less physical vitality." There might be challenging moments where we seem to, but overall, these moments are transient.

Constraining and lopsided emotional moments are always transient. But true and divinely balanced love is eternal and empowering. It is this loving and expanding essence that awakens our awareness and potential to the infinite. In fact, we have an immortal calling to grow in all of the above areas including our mortal body. But we are also connected to our true immortal self, or soul, through love. We have a yearning, a calling, a vision, and a message inside us to expand ourselves towards the infinite. In his essay *Circles*, Ralph Waldo Emerson says, "Our soul calls us to ever greater circles, but the mind with its belief systems hems us in, until a greater idea from a more universal mind is brought to our awareness, and then the boundary of our mind unfolds to an ever greater boundary, and that, without end, ad infinitum."

Our mind is called to explore the infinity of divinity in all aspects of our life, to expand our existence, and to awaken our essence. Because of the void that drives the value to explore and to expand, we have a value on searching – or at least on recollecting what we innately know. Our voids determine our values, and what's perceived most missing becomes most important. For example, if we perceive ourselves not having a relationship, we seek one. If we perceive ourselves having less money than we desire, we seek more. If we perceive ourselves not having knowledge, we seek it. Whatever we perceive as most missing drives us into seeking what we imagine to be important. We import it into our awareness, so that we may climb the next rung on the great ladder of awareness. We are constantly expanding ourselves, and our voids in the infinite are driving our values in the finite, and the very word "fulfillment" means "filling full the mind". It was Henry James who said, "Nothing of the senses will ever satisfy the soul." The only things that will satisfy the soul are gratitude and love of the heart. Our yearnings are driving our values; our values are dictating our destiny; our destinies are changing with our changing values; our destiny is just a destination in space and time along our journey and our journey is a summation of all our destinies.

Can you see the holiness in those things you take for granted – a paved road or a washing machine? If you concentrate on finding what is 'good' in every situation, you will discover that your life will suddenly be filled with gratitude, a feeling that nurtures the soul.

– RABBI HAROLD KUSHNER

Each one of us has a unique hierarchy of values, and what's most important to me may be least important to you. As a result, we see the world differently. Imagine a husband and wife walking through the mall. Her highest value is her children – their clothes, health, education, etc. His highest value is his business. As they walk through the mall, she will notice things related to children and will hardly pay attention to anything in the business section. She will have "attention surplus order" in the children's department, and "attention deficit disorder" when it comes to browsing the business section. In turn, he won't notice things in the children's department, but will focus on business. He will have "attention surplus order" when it comes to things related to business, and "attention deficit disorder" when it comes to kids' stuff. As a result, when he is shopping, she shuts down, and when she is shopping, he starts snoring. In order to salvage this situation, God has sent Starbucks to

Earth in the middle of the mall, to keep them awake, so they can appreciate each other.

Here is the paradox. Whatever is lowest on our value list is often our most disowned part. And whatever we disown, we attract into our life again and again through others, until we learn to love and own it. Whenever something supports our values, we open up to it and let it in. But whenever it challenges our values, we push it away. So what he is pushing away, she may be letting in, and vise versa. This is just a game we play. He becomes awake to and sees opportunities in whatever supports his values. Just like researchers do. When they are researching something, they will let in stuff that supports their values or beliefs, but they will tend to close off to things that go against their values.

Evaluation Trap, or Where Shall I Put You?

He who is different from me does not impoverish me –
he enriches me. Our unity is constituted in
something higher than ourselves – in Man ...
For no man seeks to hear his own echo,
or to find his reflection in the glass.
– ANTOINE DE SAINT-EXUPERY

As we go through life projecting our values onto our immediate world and the universe, we evaluate everything, and in the process, we polarize the unpolarizable and humanize the infinite divine. We project our values and assume that everyone sees the world through our eyes. We are also unwisely trying to avoid half the equation, that is, anything that challenges our values. When we see someone who supports our values, we put him/her up on a pedestal, and when we see someone who challenges us, we put him/her into a pit. By doing so, we sentence ourselves to having lives filled with infatuations and admiration, or resentments and disdain.

But when we put people on pedestals, they occupy time and space in our mind. And if you have ever been infatuated, you'll know that it's hard to get them out of your mind. This unbalanced perception automatically creates a bondage attachment to the object of our infatuation. We only see the positive, we are attracted to it, and it runs our life. At the same time, if we see something that really challenges us, we label it "bad" and want to avoid it. But the fact is that what we resent also occupies space and time in our mind.

The truth of the matter is that anytime we evaluate something, we become consumed by an illusion of something above or below us. If we are infatuated with someone, we want to sacrifice ourselves for that person. We minimize our own values and inject his/her values into our life. We want to change ourselves to be more like this person. Precisely at that moment we become ungrateful for who we are. People we put on pedestals lead us to ingratitude for our own existence. And, because we perceive them having something we don't, we disown parts of ourselves. Believe me, they don't have something we don't. They just have it in a different form. And if we minimize ourselves and want to change ourselves into them, we'll be living someone else's life. We'll be living with shoulds and ought tos, got tos, have tos, and supposed tos, and all those imperatives of someone else's making.

At the same time, if we get self-righteous or cocky because someone is challenging our values, we put him/her down in a pit and get resentful. Now we go around with our own shoulds and ought tos, got tos, have tos, and supposed tos, etc. We get puffed up and inflated with self-righteousness. We impose our imperatives on others and want to change them to be more like us. That's the moment we become ungrateful for them. Every time we exaggerate or minimize others, we automatically bring a state of ingratitude into our life. We want to be like someone else, or we want others to be like us, but how many of us just want to be loved and appreciated for who we are?

Do not fear mistakes – there are none.
– MILES DAVIS

When we love people for who they are, they turn into the ones we love. But as long as we have an imbalanced perspective we spend an awful lot of energy building pedestals and digging pits. The funny thing is that we are absolutely sure our judgment is right. This is where human will defies divine will. This entire evaluation process emerged from an assumption that there is something missing in the first place. And as long as we identify with our finite, mortal sensory being, we will have this void and value axis. In a state of ingratitude, we want to judge ourselves and others. But if we humble ourselves to the infinite potential that lies within us, we will realize that nothing is missing. It's just in the form that we have yet to recognize. Once we do, we see that the void was just an illusion, and the value we are seeking is already there in its full potential.

There is nothing to judge or evaluate any more. Our mind is perfectly balanced. We see that everything is in order, we stop our evaluation, and we enter into the world of the S.O.U.L., the Spirit Of Unconditional Love. In this state, there is no judgment, just an embrace of the divine magnificence in others, as well as non-denial of divinity in ourselves. In that moment, our unconditional love and our gratitude are overwhelming, and we are able to see what is, instead of projecting what isn't, and we are able to honour the presence of the previously hidden divine order.

What's my Purpose in Life, and How do I Live a Life of Purpose?

Here is the test to find whether your mission on Earth is finished: if you're alive, it isn't.
– *RICHARD BACH*

At seventeen, when I was living in a tent in Hawaii and surfing every day, I almost died of strychnine poisoning. This unexpected crisis turned into a great blessing though when I had the great fortune of meeting a wise man named Paul C. Bragg who helped me awaken to my life's inspiring mission. This mission or dream was to become a great teacher, healer, and philosopher. I wanted to travel the world and dedicate my life to the study of the universal laws as they relate to body, mind and spirit – particularly as they relate to healing. I wanted to go to every country in the world and share my research findings with people. I wanted to help them live their most inspired and magnificent lives. This is what I set out to do when I was seventeen, and I've been working on it for thirty-four years. I'm still working on this mission, and I intend to continue working on it as long as my physical body is alive. I've been blessed to share this message with over one and half billion people now. I have come to believe that there's nothing but divine love and all else is just an illusion. I now say, "Where is love not, and where is God not?" Anything we cannot describe as an expression of divinity and love is something we have not yet fully come to know. It guides us through natural feedback systems to bring our perceptions back into balance so that we may recognize the divine order in it.

When I was eighteen years old, I had the great opportunity to read A Discourse on Metaphysics written by the German philosopher Gottfried Wilhelm Leibniz. In it, he beautifully described what he called divine perfection, divine beauty, divine love, and the divine magnificence. He stated that few people have ever got to know what true divine perfection is, but those who have – their lives were changed forever. I believe that those who are inspired to probe deeper, beyond their own initial evaluations, and those who humble themselves to their inner voice and inner vision, can experience their truest divine nature – their true loving spirit that radiates inside each one of us.

The tragedy of life is not that it ends so soon,
but that we wait so long to begin it.
– *W. M. LEWIS*

Since I was eighteen, I also wanted to be one of those people Leibniz wrote about. I wanted to know how to awaken to, and capture, a higher awareness of this divine love and magnificence. Those who don't recognize and acknowledge it go through life evaluating and missing it. Because of our ungrateful biases, our physical bodies respond with reactions called stress. Eventually, our bodies break down, and the very atoms they are composed of are utilized by those who discover this great truth. Our physical symptoms are nothing but our body's feedback system to our conscious mind trying to awaken it to the truth of the divine perfection and ever present love. When we are awakened and know how to decipher those signs, we are guided back to the truth of our heart. The truth allows us not to evaluate, but to soulfully e-LOVE-u-ate, and in the process we are able to embody the love as light.

When we have a positive or negative bias, when we are infatuated or resentful, we have gravitating emotions that weigh us down. But when we bring our biases back into balance and equilibrium, we integrate both sides of our lopsided emotions into a moment of divine enlightenment. This enlightening radiation expands us to the ever-greater concentric circles or spheres as our soul calls us to our more masterful and expanded destiny. If we master the art of living in the loving present by looking at the balance of life, we awaken our soulful, guiding, divine principle that destines us for greatness – we awaken the Gratitude Effect.

The Ripple Effect

If God is omnipotent, and omniscient, and omnipresent, then every human action and reaction, every human aspiration and feeling is part of divinity.

– *ALBERT EINSTEIN*

When we ignore the gratitude principle and don't look deep enough, we judge and label things right away. But a week, a month, a year, or five years later, we realize that our judgment was just an imbalanced illusion.

For thirty-four years, I've kept a daily record of what I have been grateful for. I haven't missed a day. My point is that if we look, there are so many things throughout the day we can be grateful for. But if we are only looking for the things that support us, and not honour the things that challenge us, we miss the balanced magnificence of it all. Then we cannot have true fulfillment – we have "half-fillment", searching for only half of the equation. It's like searching for a one-sided magnet instead of embracing the magnetism that opportunities are drawn to us through. If we embrace both sides of life, the support and the challenge, then we get to embrace our wholeness. So, for thirty-four years I have been working on gratefully acknowledging what truly is. This is source of the Gratitude Effect.

We make our world significant by the courage of our questions and by the depth of our answers.

– *CARL SAGAN*

If we don't see the order right away, it's our responsibility to keep looking. When we are humbled to divinity and see the divine magnificence, in that moment of gratitude, we are catapulted to a new quantum level with the power of the Gratitude Effect. We are transformed by our willingness to be receptive to the divine intelligence and order. I think, our liberty in life, our freedom from the bondages of misperception is granted the moment we are humbled to the divine order and the universal laws that are guiding us. In that moment of gratitude, we acknowledge our own lasting magnificence instead of focusing on our mortal insignificance.

I've spent the last thirty-four years attempting to develop a reproducible science to help people recognize themselves in all human beings. I realized a long time ago that no matter what anyone says about me, it's true. I own it all. I'm nice, and I'm mean; I'm kind, and I'm cruel; I'm giving, but I'm also taking. I can deny half of it and pretend it belongs to others, but when I'm honest, I discover that I have it all. I used to think that I wanted to get rid of half of it. Then I realized that it was futile. It kept surfacing in my life over and over again. Finally, I started to embrace it. And the moment I did, I learnt to use it wisely. I guess my point is that you don't have to get rid of any part of yourself in order to love yourself. You are magnificent just the way you are. You were created in awe. If anything in you hadn't served some purpose, it would've been extinct. But it's there. And if we don't see how it serves, it's our job to continue looking. May we never give up on our search; for, with this discovery comes the Gratitude Effect.

I was told in the first grade that I would never be able to read, write, or communicate. I was told that I would never amount to anything and never go too far in life. I believed it. For ten years, from the age of seven to seventeen, I believed it. At seventeen, I met Paul C. Bragg who believed that I was a genius and could apply my wisdom. And his certainty was greater than my doubt. His clarity transformed my awareness of myself, and my destiny. Ever since meeting that wise man, I've dreamed of doing the same for people across the world. I believed that I could transform their lives because I watched how this belief has transformed mine.

I think it's wise to take a moment each day, before you go into the dream world, to be grateful for whatever you had experienced during the day. It's also wise to start your day with gratitude when you come out of the nightly dream world and enter into this day time dream adventure. It's all a dream world, and gratitude is the essence. Gratitude has a ripple effect in all areas of our lives. And our real power in life is awakened through gratitude and its effect called love. When we are ungrateful, we close our life down in fear and guilt; but when we are filled with gratitude, events that some call miracles happen. In the following chapters, I would like to share with you how gratitude can be a guiding light in your spiritual quest, how it can affect your mind, your career, and your finances. I would also like to show you what the Gratitude Effect can do for your family, your social relationships, and your physical well-being. So, buckle up. Let's start the journey.

If the only prayer you said in your whole life was
"thank you," that would suffice.
– MEISTER ECKHART

CHAPTER 2

Gratitude and Your Spiritual Quest

God is a metaphor for a mystery that absolutely transcends all human categories of thought, including being and non-being.
– *JOSEPH CAMPBELL*

How Can I be Grateful When God has Abandoned Me?

God is a circle whose centre is everywhere, and whose circumference is nowhere.
– *ARISTOTLE*

I would love to start our conversation about spirituality with a story of a lovely lady I'll call Linda whom I met at one of my seminars. Linda had a son who loved racing motorcycles and dirt bikes when he was a teenager. He was completely dedicated to his sport, but Linda was anxious about it because it was quite dangerous. At the same time, she was invigorated by her son's achievements. He really excelled at his sport, learnt to do amazing things on dirt bikes, became a leading contender, was winning major contests, and then one day he had a serious accident. Nobody knew if he was going to make it. It was a very close call. The accident didn't kill him, but chances were that he could be partly paralyzed for the rest of his life.

Before the accident, Linda often prayed to God that her son would be kept safe and yet also excel at his sport. She had an exaggerated, unrealistic expectation or fantasy of what her son was supposed to accomplish, and of what God was supposed to do to protect him. She was asking, yet at the same time telling God (or whatever her conception and projection of God was at the time) what to do.

When her son became injured, Linda was devastated. She became angry and bitter, and she blamed God for the accident. She was outraged that He could let this happen. She went from her fantasy expectation into a major depression. She lived with this depression for years. It was not for quite some time before she and her son came to one of my seminars entitled The Breakthrough Experience. At the seminar, I was able to completely turn around her perception of the accident and have her experience the Gratitude Effect. Here's how.

When her son was trying different treatments for his injuries initially, he went to a chiropractor who helped him make major improvements and regain some of his functions. As a result, he decided to become a chiropractor himself. So he furthered his education, eventually graduating as a Doctor of Chiropractic. Over time, excelled in his practice. He once again became a high achiever, serving many patients and becoming quite rich. He recovered from his injuries almost fully, specialized in patients who were dirt bike racers, and, on top of being a doctor, he eventually opened his own dirt bike company. Had it not been for this injury, he wouldn't have become a Doctor of Chiropractic, wouldn't have found his new path, wouldn't have become a healer with a great heart to serve people, and wouldn't have had the money to buy his dirt bike company. When Linda saw that, she said, "Oh, my God, this actually turned out to be a truly great blessing!" So her anxiety about him killing himself was transformed. She saw that his injury led him to a new path of discovering his healing power, which, in turn, led him to even greater achievements in life and on to an even greater form of his original racing dream.

At first, Linda was bitter and angry with God, and she didn't see the hidden divine order in the situation, but the seeds of the blessings were always there. So, Linda came full circle, realizing that a higher design had fulfilled both of her dreams. Once she saw her son's experience this way, she had tears of gratitude in her eyes, and she said, "Now I see the blessings. I am very grateful, and I thank God for letting this happen. I actually see that there was a hidden order, and I don't know if I would have wanted to live the rest of my life worrying whether he was going to have his neck broken. I got both my wishes and prayers taken care of." Initially after the injury, Linda was angry with God, thinking that somehow He had made a mistake, when in fact, everything was in perfect divine order from the very beginning. Where is divine order not? Where is love not?

Some people grumble because roses have thorns;
I am thankful that the thorns have roses.
– ALPHONSE KARR

No matter what happens in your life, be sure to count your blessings because any crisis always has within it a hidden blessing if you take the time to look a little closer. When you don't see the blessing, it's your choice. I believe that there's never a crisis without a blessing, there's never a loss without a gain, there's never a window shut without a new window opened, and there's never a tragedy without something we later laugh about, a comedy of a sort. It's wise to look for the synchronous blessing and be grateful from the very beginning and not wait. Instead of having the wisdom of the ages with the aging process, I encourage people to open up to the wisdom of the ages without the aging process. The Gratitude Effect is having the wisdom to see the hidden order in the apparent chaos of all of life's events and being grateful now.

When people get angry with God for not answering their appealing prayers, they are projecting their own fantasies and human-willed expectations on Him. Even having God being limited to a Him is possibly an idea worth pondering. And if God didn't match people's expectations and didn't do everything they asked Him to do, they become angry with Him. I think this is foolishness, not wisdom. Wisdom is seeing the hidden magnificence, and knowing that there's nothing out of order in the first place. True gratitude is being grateful for the order – for what is, as it is. And why wait? Just look for it – it's always there. Wisdom is the instantaneous recognition that a crisis is a blessing.

Is There a Higher Order or Plan?

When the heart has acquired stillness, it will look upon the heights and depths of knowledge, and the intellect, once quieted, will be given to hear wonderful things from God.

– *HESYCHIOS THE MARTYR*

Since the beginning of time, people have wanted to understand the world around them. Primitive mythological beliefs were the first attempts to satisfy human curiosity and to make sense of what people observed around them. Later, mythology gave birth to religion and science. Eventually people came to realize an inherent natural order in everything. It is the sense of awe for this hidden intelligent universal order that provided the great minds of the past with strength and conviction to look into the unknown and to make their great discoveries, to remain true to their quest, and to do so in spite of the countless challenges and setbacks they faced.

As I have already mentioned, when I was eighteen years old, I was profoundly affected by the book called *Discourse of Metaphysics* by G. W. Leibniz. In his inspiring text, Leibniz, the great mathematician, theologian and scientist, discussed what he called life's underlying divine perfection and order. When I read his words, my heart opened, and I became inspired. Tears ran down my face in gratitude for its awakening. From that moment on I began searching for ways to unveil this hidden order. It seemed at first that that so few ever seem to be awakened to it. The more I investigated the universe, the more I became aware of this order. It is inherent, though often latent, within our hearts and minds.

Often the scientific method falls short in explaining complex phenomena. In cases involving a large number of variables, the invisible laws of the universe become almost inaccessible. Yet, amid the apparent chaos, there remains a hidden order that often escapes human perception. The moment inquisitive minds see this hidden order, they grow stronger in their conviction that there is a divinely organized intelligence managing the world.

While conducting thousands of consultations over the last twenty years, I have helped people discover the hidden order in their lives. When they discover this beautiful perfection, they experience an epiphany and humbleness. It is as if they commune with a hidden intelligence that seems to them to be the source of this order. And anyone who has had the intense experience of discovering this hidden order is moved by profound reverence for the Grand Organized Design. Through this powerful understanding, anyone can achieve liberation from the shackles of personal fantasies and unrealistic desires, and attain this humble attitude of mind toward the grandeur of reason behind their intelligently governed existence. This attitude is in essence a true religiosity – a deep appreciation of an awe-inspiring intelligence. The individuals to whom we owe the greatest creative achievements of science all shared the truly religious conviction that this universe is perfect in its divine order and open to understanding and wisdom. They know that in actuality there is nothing but love. This love is the essence of the Gratitude Effect.

My Box is Better Than Yours

Arguing about whether or not God exists is like fleas arguing about whether the dog exists; arguing about God's correct name is like fleas arguing about the name of the dog; and arguing over whose notion of God is correct is like fleas arguing about who owns the dog.

– *ROBERT FULGHUM*

Let's talk about boxes. What do they have to do with spirituality, you ask? Well, many of us use our little boxes to house our ideas and, sadly, our stereotypes of spirituality. Let me share a story with you.

At one of my seminars, a woman came to me and said, "My husband, he is just not spiritual."

And I said, "What do you mean, he's not spiritual?"

"Well, he just doesn't believe in God. And he doesn't believe in going to church."

I asked her, "Do you think your husband is an atheist? Is he denying God?"

"Yes."

"Alright. I have a question for you. What exactly does spirituality mean to you? What do you think spirituality represents and consists of?"

"Well, to believe in God. You've got to do that!"

I said, "You've got to do that? 'Got to' usually implies something on the outside telling you what to do. Where did you get that idea?"

"Well, I guess, I was taught that."

We started probing into her life, and she realized that she subordinated herself to the belief and authority system of her religion. This is not bad or good; it's just that she didn't really take the time to ask whether this belief had any meaning to her personally. She was just parroting something she was told to do. She did not take the time to contemplate what the word "God" meant to her.

Then I asked her, "Even though your husband claims to be an atheist, what does he do that is spiritual?"

"Well, nothing. He doesn't do anything spiritual."

I asked her, "Do you think that you are possibly limiting your belief about what spirituality is? Are you limiting your concepts of spirituality to only the acts of praying, or going to church? What about before there was a church of your faith, and before people knew to follow such traditional rituals? What are a few alternative or possibly broader ways of expressing spirituality? Does he go to work? Does he earn a living?

"Yes."

"Does that help you raise your family financially? Is that a loving service that could be considered an act of spirituality?"

"Well, yes."

"So, does he possibly have some of his own actions or objectives that could be considered spiritual?"

"I guess, you can say that."

I said, "Does he bring a service to the world?"

"Yes."

"Does he help a lot of people with it?"

"Oh, millions of people."

"So, he is out there providing a service to millions of people, and is that not a spiritual contribution?"

"Well... I guess... If you put it that way, then it is."

I said, "Does he love his work?"

"Yes, he's definitely dedicated to his work."

"His dedication and love of what he's doing, isn't that a spiritual service too? Do you think that a person who doesn't love what he is doing but goes to church is somehow more spiritual than the person who loves what he's doing and is dedicated to his work that serves millions of people? Is this more or less spirituality?"

"Well, I haven't thought of it this way. I guess that's probably just as spiritual."

I said, "Does he love his family? Does he care about the kids?"

"Yes."

"Is that spiritual?"

"I guess so."

"And he provides for them and helps them grow?"

"Yes."

"He helps them with their education?"

"Yes."

"Is that spiritual? Is that something of value?"

"Yes."

"If he suddenly died today, would any of those things be a challenge to you? And would you, then, not be able to go to church? Would you then have to focus on all those other things he did as an act of love for your kids?"

"Yes."

"And wouldn't that be spiritual?"

"Yes."

I said, "Are you sure you haven't boxed in what spirituality is? Maybe, he doesn't believe in your kind of spirituality, but does this mean he is not spiritual? Maybe, he doesn't buy the anthropocentric projection of what you think God is. Maybe he sees nature or the order of the universe as something to appreciate, worship and to honour?

She says, "Well, that's what he does; he is a scientist. He studies the laws of nature."

I said, "Well, how do you know that that's not as much spirituality as yours?"

The astronomer Carl Sagan once wrote, "But I see the emergence in our consciousness of a universe of magnificence, and an intricate, elegant order far beyond anything our ancestors imagined. And if much about the universe can be understood in terms of a few simple laws of Nature, those wishing to believe in God can certainly ascribe those beautiful laws to a reason underpinning all of Nature. My own view is that it is far better to understand the Universe as it really is than to pretend to a universe as we might wish it to be."

Your neighbor's vision is as true for him as your own vision is true for you.
– *MIGUEL DE UNAMUNO*

Some people have this belief that their idea of spirituality is the only one that's right, but what if nobody's spiritual quest was right or wrong. Thank God, everyone is unique. By the way, I'd love to transform the term GOD into an acronym standing for the impersonal Grand Organized Design of the universe or the personal Grand Organizing Designer, or possibly the Great Organizing Director. Our concepts of spirituality eventually collectively overlap, and we are here to learn to love all of them.

No exception. Anyone, whom we can't love or be grateful for, shows us the boundaries of our box.

For each one of us, there is someone in the world with the exact opposite of our values. We are all entangled, just like particles and antiparticles or positrons and "negatrons" (electrons) are entangled in quantum physics as complementary opposites. For every two people who have a reverse value system, one is labelled negative, and the other one – positive. One man's poison is another man's food. And the summation of all the values in the world balances itself out to create the divine order of love. That's the love of the world. That's God's love if you want to call it that – the Grand Organized Design's love of the world. And everyone we attract into our life, with similar or different values, is there to teach us to love it all. Any part we can't love is the part that stagnates us, constricts us, and blocks us from loving the disowned part of ourselves. Every human being has every human trait, and learning how to love all the different people and all the different value systems is the journey that's ultimately about loving ourselves. We are here to learn to love it all.

I believe that no matter what you've done or not done, you are worthy of love. No matter what you've done or not done, you are participating in the global equilibrium that is ultimately divine love. Over the years, I've developed The Demartini Method®, whose objective is to help receptive people see the hidden perfection in their life, and to see that there's nothing to change in themselves or others. We are here to learn to love and be grateful. This doesn't mean that we will stay in the state of love and gratitude forever. It means that once we see the order, we are promoted to the next thing we don't love yet. Once we learn to love that, we are promoted to the next level, and we get to learn again. So, we get to grow indefinitely, and at every stage, we have the opportunity to rediscover the hidden order that's always there. And this impacts us and everyone around us through unleashing the Gratitude Effect.

Where Is God Not?

As I make my slow pilgrimage through the world, a certain sense of beautiful mystery seems to gather and grow.
– A. C. BENSON

The following story will tell you for sure if your notion of GOD is boxed in. The founder of the Sikh religion was a great teacher named Guru Nanak. He was truly a man who dedicated his life to the study of the religions of the world. In his quest, he went to Israel and studied Judaism and Christianity, and he journeyed to Mecca to study Mohammed's teachings. He went to the Kaaba, which is a cubical building in the centre of the big square in Mecca, and on the eastern wall of the Kaaba, there is a sacred stone, a meteorite set into the wall.

He walked into the square and lay down on his back in meditation with his feet toward the sacred stone. But the rule of the temple was that you never point your feet in the direction of the sacred stone. You are only to bow down to it because it is a symbol of Allah, and the feet are considered unclean. Everybody kneels down and faces it in a great circle, and anyone who reverses that is a blasphemer. He lay down that way and the Muslims around him were deeply offended.

They cried out in their language, "Blasphemy! Blasphemy! How dare you put your feet toward the sacred stone?"

They pushed his feet away, but he just spun around, and his feet were magically brought back to the stone. They kicked him, but he rolled and sat up again, facing the same way. They dragged him out, but he just followed them back in. No matter what they did, his feet would return toward the stone like a compass needle. Nothing they did seemed to make the slightest difference. He kept his feet pointing to the stone. Everyone was with him. He finally asked them, "Brothers, why are you so upset?"

"Because you put your feet toward the sacred stone!"

"And why is that so terrible?"

"Because the sacred stone represents God, and you don't put your feet in the direction of God. That is bad!"

He said, "If you can tell me where God is not, I will gladly put my feet there."

There are three thousand religions, and spirituality is not about being exclusive. It's not limited to any one of those religions. Instead, it includes all of them and even more. Although atheism is the denial of theism, it can't exist without first acknowledging it. Sometimes, the actions of people who are believers are atheistic. They tell God what to do; they say in their prayers, "Here's what I want." Then they expect God to follow their command. This is atheistic, if not plain foolish. No matter what religion you practise, you are a part of a bigger spiritual picture.

If you desire to love yourself, others, and the experience of life more, being grateful for the gift of life is one of the most important steps you can take towards living the life of your dreams. And it doesn't matter if you are more conventional in your spiritual beliefs or less orthodox, you can still constantly remain grateful for the invisible energy flow of life that surrounds and fills you – the energy that some call the soul, others – holy spirit, and still others, life force. Do not underestimate the depth of gratitude that you will experience by connecting to your own form of higher forces. Do not underestimate the power of the Gratitude Effect. Taking this one step can have an amazing effect on all the seven areas of your life.

How Can I Be Grateful for the Evil in the World?

If only there were evil people somewhere insidiously committing evil deeds, and it were necessary only to separate them from the rest of us and destroy them. But the line dividing good and evil cuts through the heart of every human being.

– *ALEXANDR SOLZHENITSYN*

Most people would agree that gratitude works well in almost any life situation, but the question of "evil" throws many of them off. Here is my take on it. Your highest value serves as an expression of your spirituality. Say, your highest value is your children. You will feel that the universe is working with you to help you find fulfillment in this area. It becomes your spiritual mission. Take Rose Kennedy's mission, for example: "I dedicate my life to raising a family of world leaders." But a person, whose highest value is physical fitness, may worship the body as a temple of the spirit, do yoga, work out, etc. This may be his/her spiritual quest. A person who loves to go to church may think that tradition and religion are his/her spiritual quest. A person, who values work, may see developing his/her company that serves millions of people as a spiritual quest. A philanthropist builds wealth and serves the world that way, thinking that's his/her spiritual quest.

Our spirituality is expressed through the hierarchy of our values that are as unique as our fingerprints. They are based on our experiences, and, since there can never be two people with exactly the same experience, there are no two people who have the same spiritual awareness. Because of our uniqueness, anything that supports our values, we label "good", and anything that challenges our values, we label "bad" or "evil." We are constantly judging and labelling the world around us, filtering things through our value system. Well, so is everybody else.

The great awareness comes slowly, piece by piece.
The path of spiritual growth is a path of lifelong learning.
The experience of spiritual power is basically a joyful one.
– *M SCOTT PECK*

It truly is a paradox – those who seek God the most are often the ones who deny His presence the most because they assume Divinity is not already here in everything. Like a fish unaware of the water it lives in, we often take the divine nature of our existence for granted. It's our job to look beyond our illusions and myths to find the underlying truth. It is incredible how many people go off on a quest to find divinity, but in the end, they look back and realize that it was there all along.

I suggest that the shining light of Divinity is something beyond all religious belief systems on this planet. It is greater than anybody's interpretation or perception of it. It's a source of energy, literally, a cosmic particle ray system that bombards us like photons coming from outer space. It illuminates and guides our life when we are open and receptive. It is infinitely powerful, and we are completely permeated by it. This extraordinary and intense spiritual force physically and metaphysically fills and governs us. The more balanced our mind is, and the more open our heart is, the higher the frequency and energy of this force. This orderly force is the balanced energy of true divine love. It constantly whispers its wholeness by awakening within us the Gratitude Effect.

Human beings, vegetables, or cosmic dust – we all dance to a mysterious tune, intoned in the distance by an invisible piper.
– *ALBERT EINSTEIN*

I think that true spirituality is an expression of our S.O.U.L, the Spirit Of Unconditional Love. When we have a moment of unconditional love, when we don't project our limiting and filtering values but dissolve them for an instant, we see things as they are, and we become one with our soul. We become one with our collective essence, not just our selective existence. That's when we more fully awaken our spiritual expression.

When we judge things and polarize things, we experience the terrestrial world. I call it the trial world - the terresTRIAL world. When we are in our soul, we are in the celestial, harmonious world. When we are grateful for the ordered harmony, we have access to the instantaneous wisdom of our soul and we continue to make quantum leaps and grow. Anytime we are grateful, we expand, evolve and grow. It's automatic. And every time we are ungrateful for anything, we undergo a constraining revolution. We are here to learn to love it all. And if we resist loving something, we'll keep revolving and dealing with it, and revolving and dealing with it again, until we learn to love it. And when we do, we get to evolve again. So we go through cycles of revolution when we are ungrateful, and we undergo quantum leaps of evolution when we are grateful.

Our essence is to grow. It's a yearning inside our hearts. Our spiritual quest is unique. But so is everyone else's. They are here to teach us how to love all parts of ourselves. And it's not limited to people. We are here to learn to love it all – events, social systems, classes, colours, races, ages, genders, etc. There's nothing unworthy of love. If you see a big enough picture, you will see that even peace and war, the kind and the cruel all fit in the picture. We can't exclude anything. Out of our ignorance, we have attempted to do it, but it's not wise because it's not doable. Whatever we resist persists.

Anything in which we don't see the divine order becomes a mystery. Everything in which we have seen the order is now history. We are here to grow into the greater levels of mystery and to discover the universal intelligence with its divine order in all things. Anything that is balanced in our perspective evokes gratitude. We learn eventually that any imbalance was just an illusion. We realize that there were no mistakes. It's all been in divine order always.

There is nothing but Love. All else is illusion.
– DR DEMARTINI

There are no Miracles for Those that Have no Faith in Them

Faith is taking the first step even when you don't see the whole staircase
– MARTIN LUTHER KING, JR

I want to tell you the story of Mikey. It's a story of faith that was challenged but then deepened and strengthened as a direct result of that challenge. I was in my first year of chiropractic practice. A gentleman came in with a workers' compensation case. He injured himself at work by twisting his body. His spine got injured, a number of muscles were pulled, and some of his bones were out of place. I started adjusting him, and he was recovering very well. After a week or two, he was able to function normally. He was so grateful that he asked me if he could bring his wife in for a consultation.

I said, "Absolutely, and you are welcome to bring in your children too. I would be honoured to do an exam on them and make sure their spines are aligned and functioning soundly."

He said, "Great, but one of my kids has a problem that you won't be able to help."

I asked, "What do you mean?"

"He was in a serious car accident when he was a baby, and he's had some deforming injuries and some severe problems since that time."

"What happened?"

"We were going about seventy miles an hour, and we had a head-on collision. He was thrown about seventy feet into the air and came down onto the road. His leg was turned in; he cut his face, broke his pelvis and became blind in his right eye. "Has he seen a chiropractor?"

"No, but he is going to an occupational therapist."

I said, "When you bring your wife tomorrow, bring him in, just in case there is something I can do. Let me just look at him."

The next day, he brought his wife and his son in. His son's name was Mikey. The wife was getting an exam in the next room with my assistant, and Mikey and his father were in another room with me.

As I was examining this boy, I noticed that he had a lot of injuries to his neck, some of his vertebrae were out of alignment, and his pelvis was definitely way out of position; he had a big scar across his face, and his eye didn't move. I was feeling the back of his skull with my fingers and I realized that the top three of his vertebrae were out of position and his brain pulse was not synchronized. Whenever I see that, I know that the brain can't function fully. I adjusted the three vertebrae back into place and focused my attention on synchronizing his brain pulse. I adjusted his neck, and then I closed my eyes holding his neck in my hands waiting for the synchronization to occur.

His father was at the feet of the child. Suddenly, he cried, "Oh, my God! Oh, my God! Sherry, Sherry! Come quick!" Sherry was the name of his wife. She got off the table in the back room and came running into the room. Mikey's eye had moved. It opened up and was looking directly at them. All of us got chills up our spines. His parents were both sitting on the floor at his feet in tears of gratitude. A second later, we realized that his sight had actually come back at that moment.

We started talking, and his parents kept saying, "It's a miracle, it's a miracle. If this is possible, what else is possible?" They were asking me if I thought he would be able to function normally again, and the three of us were busy talking and not paying attention to Mikey who was lying on the table. Because he had been immobilized his whole life, there was no danger in leaving him on the table like that, or so we thought.

Listen to this. While we were talking, he rolled off the table and came down onto his leg that was turned in and fell against the wall. But before he fell, he landed on his feet, and for one short second, he stood. He had never been able to do this in his entire life until that moment.

I started working with this boy adjusting his spine and his pelvis, and gradually his motion improved, and his eyesight returned permanently. His parents put him in skateboarding elbow pads, kneepads, wrist pads, and a helmet as he learnt to walk. After three months of frequent visits to my office, he was able to walk down the hallway on his own without falling once. Soon little Mikey was able to walk without his helmet, kneepads or elbow pads.

Faith is knowledge within the heart, beyond the reach of proof.
– *KAHLIL GIBRAN*

Mikey's parents were told that he would be handicapped for the rest of his life, and wouldn't see or walk. Every time we made progress, it brought tears of gratitude in his parents' and my eyes. We were all grateful to see this miracle unfold, and I was very grateful to be a part of his recovery. I learnt to never give up on something. If someone tells you it can't happen, it doesn't mean that it won't. You have to set up reasonable expectations, but I just don't know what they are when it comes to healing. I've seen so many things, others would call miracles, happen.

I just know that as we were grateful for each stage of the progress, the recovery kept happening. The more grateful we were, the more progress he made. That family experienced the Gratitude Effect first hand. At first, they didn't believe that his recovery was possible. But because I did and told them to bring

Mikey in, they took a risk and they trusted me. I am grateful for this case because it taught me to have faith and certainty with patients. After Mikey I never gave up. There were hundreds of patients after Mikey that I wouldn't have pushed beyond their limits, had it not been for him. I refused to see the impossibility of their recovery, and my faith translated into their faith, and then recovery and a sense of wonder and gratitude.

We have to be willing to go the extra mile and not give up when people say, "You can't do it." Little Mikey was four when he came to see me. He had never walked in his life, but he got on his feet in my office that day. That was the beginning of a new life for him, and for me it was another chance to see the Gratitude Effect in action.

A Grain of Mustard Seed

When you have come to the edge of all light that you know and are about to drop off into the darkness of the unknown, Faith is knowing one of two things will happen: there will be something solid to stand on or you will be taught to fly.

– *PATRICK OVERTON*

Here is another story of how faith carried me through. When I lived in Hawaii, I stayed with a religious communal group for a while. We lived on this little thin strip of beach between the Pearl City and Makaha. At night we all slept on the beach, and during the day, our job was to provide any kind of service. The belief was that if we provided service during the day, somehow at night we would be taken care of. I worked all day and I didn't get to eat all day. I spent the whole day cleaning the beach picking up trash and putting it in the trashcans or helping people on the beach with whatever they needed. At night, we had to sit and read from the Bible. If we got some food – we ate, if not – we fasted.

It was not uncommon for total strangers to provide for us. One time, at about eight at night, someone stopped by and just dropped off a bunch of food, which we finished in minutes. At another time, some people were cooking on the beach next to us. They asked us, "Where do you guys live?" We said, "Right here, on the beach." They asked, "How do you survive?" We told them about our service and our beliefs, and they said, "Well, come over, we'll cook something for you." That night we had delicious hot dogs and hamburgers, and a whole bunch of other food.

This taught me that no matter what, if you have faith, you will always make it. In the group that I lived with, people were thanking Jesus at that time, but it doesn't have to be restricted to him. You can just be thankful to life. Whenever I hitchhiked and lived on the beach or on the street, I was always somehow taken care of, and it made me think that there was a higher power there, organizing things and taking care of me. It could have been the synchronicity of my mind, but I thought that it was something bigger than that. I now know it is. I guess I learnt early about the Gratitude Effect and had an aptitude for it.

Questions to Help you Experience the Gratitude Effect

- Who in my life can I be grateful for today?
- Who has supported or challenged me in such a way that it expanded me spiritually?
- What is the most inspiring thing I've experienced today?
- Who is the most inspiring person I got to meet today?
- What experience strengthened me in my spiritual understanding?
- What spiritual principle did I get to see in action today?
- In what form was love and gratitude revealed to me today?
- What seven things can I be grateful for today in my spiritual life?

- What has allowed me to expand my view of spirituality?
- What happened to me today that made me more inclusive instead of exclusive?

Affirmations to Help you on Your Spiritual Quest

- I am forever grateful for the loving energy of life.
- I understand that everyone is expressing their spirituality in a unique way according to their values.
- I embrace the unique expressions of others' spirituality.
- I love encountering new views of spirituality that broaden my horizons.
- I am a spiritual being on a mission of love.
- No matter where I am, no matter who I'm with, I'm on my spiritual mission.
- I am grateful for both support and challenge; for, both serve me, open my heart, and help me strengthen my spiritual mission.
- I honour the divine perfection and keep my heart open to its loving beauty.
- I am nothing but light until I judge myself and become en-darkened.
- I know there is nothing but love and all else is illusion.
- What a gift my life is.
- I am the vision, God is the power, and we are the team.
- My will and divine will are one; for, they are two aspects of one light.
- I meditate in silence and hear the divine voice.
- I am humbled by the beauty and magnificence of it all.
- I am inspired. I am enthused. I am enlightened. I am immortal.
- I am an infinite being remembering to love in a finite world.
- I am loving, I am grateful, and my life is blessed.
- I am an expression of the divinity and I honour myself.

It's Your Turn now

Exercise 1. Whether you say your "gratitudes" each day, give thanks before meals, write up your wish list, tune into uplifting music, or spend some quiet time in contemplation or meditation, a little time spent partaking in a daily spiritual ritual is incredibly nourishing for body, mind and spirit.

Put aside a little time each and every day for connecting to the higher spiritual forces – it is amazing how wonderful you can feel when you allow yourself to open up your heart and mind to the invisible, metaphysical world. Gratitude is the key that opens up the gateway of your heart and allows your love and inspirations to shine.

Exercise 2. Each day, when you get out of bed, during your lunch period, or in the evening before you go to bed, take a moment to stop and think about what you can be grateful for. Fill your day with the Gratitude Effect. Who has contributed to your life and who can you be grateful to and love today?

In the spiritual area:

____

____

____

____

In the mental area:

____

____

____

____

____

In the vocational area:

In the financial area:

In the familial area:

In the social area:

In the physical area:

CHAPTER 3

How to Become a Genius

To believe your own thought, to believe that what is true for you in your private heart is true for all men – that is genius.
– RALPH WALDO EMERSON

The Gratitude Effect is the most powerful tool I know. Just as it will guide you on your spiritual quest, it will also help you maximize your mind's potential. So, how can you become a genius? You don't have to. You already are one. You just haven't discovered it yet. Let me show you how.

Imagine that you've been invited to a party. You go there, and you are bored out of your mind. When you leave, the person who invited you expects you to write a thank you note. You have a "socially considerate" side to your personality, so what do you do? That's right. You force yourself to write it. You start scribbling, and after a few minutes you go, "Hmm...No, that's not it..." So, you try again. You edit it over and over, but it's not flowing because it's not inspired or sincere. What can you do? You feel you need to write the damn note. So you toss it, and you start over again, and you toss it again, and you do a lot of editing until you finally give it a "it's good enough" status and you send it.

Then you go to another party, and you meet amazing people, get into inspiring discussions, learn something fascinating, forget about the time, and don't want to leave the party at all. When you go home, you write a thank you note that comes out of you and flows faster than you can write. It feels like automatic writing and just comes pouring out of you. You are truly inspired.

Inspired writing is fluent and poetic. It just comes through and flows out of your heart. It's almost like there's some force within or beyond you guiding you to write it. When we are grateful, our mind can amaze us. And I am not talking exclusively about writing. The Gratitude Effect awakens genius. It awakens mental capacities we may never have thought we had. We had them all right, but they were dormant and blocked because we were dispersing and diluting our energy on judging and evaluating. Our mind is truly powerful and works its ingenious magic when it is in the state of gratitude.

I am now going to share with you one of my simple but insightful learning shortcuts that I teach at my speed-reading and genius-awakening programme. Before you attempt to read and learn anything, stop for a moment and ask yourself the following question, "How does reading this specific material connect with my highest values, and how is it going to help me achieve my most inspiring dreams?" if you keep answering this empowering question over and over again you would eventually become utterly inspired about reading this material, and you would begin to look forward to learning even more and more about it. If you did so, your reading capacity and memory retention level would go up. And if you did not link your reading material to your highest values and did not become grateful for reading it, these new ideas would become dumped into your short-term memory at best, and before you would know it, they would fade away.

Any educational course you might attend that you feel is ultimately not helping you achieve your highest goals is one that will probably become difficult to sit in on and do well in. And when you are taking any kind of test relating to it, it's probably going to feel like a test from hell, and you are not likely to remember much of what you've learnt. Five minutes after the test, your memory will most likely go blank.

The same is the case with life in general. If you don't see how whatever you are doing is aligned to your highest values, and how it will help you fulfill your goals, both your productivity and your creativity will be hindered. Gratitude is the key that opens up the gateway of your mind and heart, and allows the genius that's inside you to be awakened. It allows your genius to bring its fullest expression to your writing, your art, your music, your singing, your business, or your performance. Anything that involves the mind is enhanced through the Gratitude Effect. Gratitude improves our attention, our retention, and our intention. Our mind maximizes its potential when we are in a state of deep appreciation. Listen to this story, and watch the Gratitude Effect in action.

Cherish your vision and your dreams as they are the children of your soul; the blueprints of your ultimate achievements.
– NAPOLEON HILL

One day, on a plane, I was sitting next to a famous singer. I can't really give away his name, but he had a famous rock band all through the seventies, eighties and early nineties. I wasn't even aware it was him because I was reading something on my computer and wasn't paying much attention. We started a simple conversation, I asked him, "Where are you from?", "What do you do?" etc. He said that he wrote music, and I asked him, "What kind of music?" And he just looked at me. He didn't know that I didn't know who he was. He finally told me who he was, and I saw his whole band sitting there next to us in the first class.

I said, "So, what's going on? What is the newest? I haven't heard of any new albums lately."

And he goes, "Well, we've been in a slump; it hasn't been really working for us lately."

I asked, "Have you had some big challenges that you have not been grateful for."

And he said, "Boy, you can say that again."

I asked, "What all has happened?"

And he tells me that they've had this happen and that happen, and more of this and of that.

I asked him, "Have you looked for the benefits of all these occurrences? There are always blessings once you truly look."

"What do you mean?"

"I mean that there are never one sided events." I began applying my Demartini Method® to his past problems right there and then, on the plane. I had to help him sort through his past challenges and discover the divine order and the blessings in everything that had happened. He understood that nothing was lost – it was simply transformed, as are all other forms of energy. We worked until he could truly see that there were great things to be thankful for arising out of the "misfortunes" he perceived and was stuck in.

The second he became grateful for everything that had happened, his eyes began to water up, and he looked at me and said, "Man, I can't believe a guy sitting next to me on a jet aeroplane just did all that."

I said, "Well, I can hardly believe I have been sitting next to a great musician. I used to listen to your music all the time." We both had a great time talking with each other, and we were both grateful for the experience.

Then I said to him, "If you close your eyes right now, focus on what you are grateful for, and ask inwardly for an inspiring new song, I'll bet that you'll receive a new song or at least a portion of it."

And he did. All of a sudden, a tear came down from his eye, and he pulled out a piece of paper and began quickly writing some lyrics down. He was really into it. I just had to leave him alone as he was letting his inspiring ideas and lyrics come through. When he became grateful, all of a sudden, his musical creativity returned. He was inspired again. But not before he broke through all this accumulated past emotional baggage that was interfering with his inner musical gift and genius. His mind was waiting to express its genius, but he had blocked it. His past and present emotional baggage had subdued him. The Gratitude Effect pulled him back up.

He could express his genius through his music again. Then he leaned over to the guys in his band who were sitting on the right behind us and said, "I think, I just got a new song."

And they go, "What?"

"This inspiring guy sitting next to me just helped me get a new song."

How to Stop Yourself from Your Greatest Achievements

We are what we think. All that we are arises with our thoughts.
With our thoughts, we make the world.
– *BUDDHA*

The musician I've just told you about stopped short of his greatest achievements by choosing the erroneous attitude. Surely, he is not alone in doing this. There are many people who are holding themselves back from expressing their fullest mental capacity because their mind is not clear. If we sort through our thoughts and discover the people, things or events we are not grateful for, then we can analyze them. We can look at our infatuations and find out what drawbacks are hidden. Then we can find the benefits of our resentments. When we are able to attain equilibrium between the positive and the negative, we return to the centre, where our mind is empowered by gratitude. The immediate experience of the Gratitude Effect is clarity of mind. We are back into lucidity. We have access to clear vision and inspiration. And whatever it is we are doing, we take it to the new level. We become congruent and more awakened. Our mind power is infinite once we recognize that a balanced state of gratitude is the source of our inspirations and true mental power. It's automatic. And the greatest of news is you don't have to believe it to try it. I suggest that you do not pass up another moment.

Our mental capacities are not limited by our formal education levels as much as they are by our perceptions and attitudes. I've seen well educated people in sports who were blocking their physical achievements and making excuses by adopting a disempowered mindset: "I'm getting too old for this. I'm nearly thirty, or forty, or fifty. There's no way I can do my sport anymore. I'm getting too old, too tired, too sick, too this or too that." These people are not truly too old, tired or sick; in most cases they have simply transformed their original inspiring vision and dreams into some other form, either temporarily or permanently. I remember this one particular gentleman who was an outstanding athlete, but had had a period of setbacks and stopped pursuing his dreams. He really didn't envision stopping that early, but after one overly challenging season, he just gave up.

I sat down with him, did my little magic, which is another word for the Demartini Method®, and was able to bring him back into a state of gratitude for his life and for what had happened during that so-called "terrible" season. He realized that the season was low because he was focused on his wife, his kids, his house, and new family developments. It wasn't a "bad" season as he first claimed, and he had not "lost" anything as he initially assumed. He simply shifted his energy and focus over into other areas of his life, and this is where he and his accomplishments grew. That's where his "success" and "gain" was. That's where his achievement was. Once he realized that, he had tears in his eyes and said to me, "Oh, my God. I didn't actually fail that year. I transformed my achievements into a different form."

I agreed, "No, you didn't fail. You didn't have a setback. You had achieved a tremendous growth in another area. You just didn't realize that your values have shifted to that area."
He asked me, "Now that those areas of my life are stable, do you really think I can become a high achiever at my sport again?"

"Absolutely," I said, "you've had the power to sustain a decent year even when you were taking on all those new family responsibilities, and you still achieved a lot. Now that those areas are stabilized, you can put your energy back into sports. You haven't "lost" anything. Your values can be readjusted back to those focused on the game."

When he became grateful for the different form of his achievement during that "terrible" season, he became grateful for himself again. Out he came again. It had nothing to do with his age. It had everything to do with his values, perceptions and resultant actions. He became a so-called "success" once more in the area of sports. He reminded me of Tiger Woods, who had a lower season when he first got married. Now his marriage is stabilized, and he's back in the game again because he redirected his values and energy. Our achievements match our values, and once we recognize this, we can awaken the Gratitude Effect.

The Answer to All Questions

We become wise when we know that love is the answer to all questions.
– DR JOHN F. DEMARTINI

When we are in a state of true gratitude and love, our mind can create what others might call "miracles". One of these apparent "miracles", which I see every week at my seminar called the Breakthrough Experience®, is the capacity of our mind to non-locally and instantly communicate with other people. You've probably noticed from your own experience that we have a stronger connection to people we are truly in love with, even if they are a thousand miles away. It's almost as if we are in sync with what's going on in their mind, and we know what they are thinking.

Local communication is limited to our senses and the speed of light. We can see and hear people we are talking to, can smell their perfume, or shake their hand. Non-local communication lies in a greater sphere of conscious awareness, which far exceeds our senses. It is instantaneous and has no boundaries. This sphere is used widely by the Tenth Degree Master Martial Artists and those more intuitive. They can be blindfolded and still be able to "protect" themselves when "attacked" by different people, although they actually perceive themselves simply "dancing" to the beat of the "attacker's invitation to dance." They can handle their so-called attackers with their eyes closed. About forty of my students and I had a chance to participate in such a Master's Martial Arts demonstration at one of my seminars in the U.S.

When we are in the state of true love and gratitude, our consciousness expands. It exceeds our sensory awareness. Our sphere of influence also expands. It means we can instantly influence people at a distance, and we can also be influenced by people from a distance if we tune in.

At one seminar in Houston, Texas, I worked with a lovely gentleman who'd had some personal problems with his sister for years, and after completing the Demartini Method®, he was flooded by the feelings of love and gratitude for her. Funny thing, the moment he broke through his despise, she called directly to the seminar room where about thirty people witnessed this "coincidence". She hadn't called or spoken to him in eleven years, but she called precisely at that moment when he overcame his resentment toward her and was hugging the surrogate person he chose to represent his sister.

The probability of that phone call coming through at that particular moment was quite low because we were in the middle of the seminar, working on top of my office in Houston, Texas after eleven o'clock on a Saturday night. For that lady to even reach me, to find my number and get through to the seminar room was very interesting. She had to call his mom, find out how to reach him, find out who knew where he was, find out the location of the seminar, find the number, etc. She had to go to a lot of trouble to reach him then and there while all of us at the seminar sat in awe over the synchronicity.

He later found out that as he was finding more and more things to be grateful for in her, she was non-locally picking up on it and she started thinking, "I need to find him and talk to him and thank him". As he became thankful for her, she simultaneously became thankful for him. They connected. This is an example of the expanding non-local sphere of awareness we have available to us when we are in the state of appreciation and begin to apply the Gratitude Effect. We can influence people no matter how far away they are from us. There is no limit to our potential when we are in a true state of openhearted gratitude. If you've never experienced this, it's worth experiencing. It is mind blowing to say the least, and it happens each week in my seminar called the Breakthrough Experience®.

What others may perceive as "miracles", are just natural laws put into operation by the power of gratitude. When you understand the laws and apply them, they might seem miraculous to someone who doesn't know the laws. The Gratitude Effect allows the mind to awaken and expand its sphere of influence and awareness. They are gifts of the open heart.

What's Your Favourite Lie?

Every man takes the limits of his own field of vision for the limits of the world.
– ARTHUR SCHOPENHAUER

Instead of awakening their genius with the Gratitude Effect, many people unwisely choose to believe limiting, self-imposed lies about themselves: "I can only remember so much, read so fast, learn so much, do so much," which is not much at all. A lie in these particular cases represents some exaggerated or minimized perception about themselves. When I was a young child, I chose to believe another sort of lie. My own story starts with a statement shared with my family by my first-grade teacher who informed us about me having reading and learning limitations when I was seven. I assumed that she was right because I didn't know any alternative at the time, I was only seven and she represented the authority that supposedly knew what she was talking about.

So, from that day on I was considered "not very bright" and "without much promise as far as academics were concerned". I was told that since my learning capacities were deficient, it would be wiser to direct my energies mainly into sports.

Ten years later I found out that with extreme persistence and dedication I could actually read and learn. The very first time I was able to read a book from cover to cover, I was very grateful and brought to tears. The story is worth telling.

I was just about to turn eighteen years of age. One afternoon, as I was leaving the small health food store called Vim and Vigor in Haleiwa, Hawaii, I saw this small greenish yellow book called *Chico's Organic Gardening and You* in the tall swivelling circular book display stand. On the cover, it had the picture of a hippie and a farmer named Chico holding up a big tomato and a pitchfork. The young man in the picture on the cover had long hair and a beard was the author of the book. I saw his picture and thought, "Hell, he looks like me. If that sucker can write this book, I bet I could read it."

That was my first book – a book written by the hippie who looked like me. It cost two dollars and seventy-five cents. To someone who had taken reading for granted, reading this book, which was mostly pictures anyway, wouldn't mean a whole lot. But, to me, it meant everything. After I finished reading it, (which really meant looking at all the garden pictures and the captions with only a small amount of text), I had tears of gratitude in my eyes. It was one of the most exhilarating moments of my life.

For ten years, I hadn't thought I could fully read, but I just discovered that I could. It meant that what I believed for ten years was untrue. This book gave me so much encouragement to continue on the path to learning.

If you are in a situation where for ten years you believed that you couldn't do something and then you realize you can, this can be a life-transforming moment. In that single moment you gain a new level of confidence.

We know what we are, but know not what we may be.

– *WILLIAM SHAKESPEARE*

After I read my first book, I went back to that health store to see if I could find another one to read. I bought Adelle Davis' book, *Let's Eat Right to Keep Fit*. I was so inspired to tackle that book, but it was overwhelming. I couldn't read that one. I set it aside. Then I found Paul Bragg's *The Miracle of Fasting Book*, and because some of the words were difficult, I wasn't able to read all of it either. That is, until during a meditation I became inspired to return to Texas to see my parents. Because the surf was subsiding on the North Shore of Oahu that spring and because I wanted to see my parents, I headed back home. I had just enough money to fly from Honolulu to Los Angeles and from there I hitchhiked back to Texas.

When I returned to my parent's home in Texas, I had my mother buy me a dictionary. I really, really, really, REALLY wanted to read. At first, I couldn't read but a few words. I had to start with dictionaries to learn how to read – first the syllables and then the more lengthy words. Then I'd use encyclopedias to learn more about those words. I had to take it one step at a time. My belief system at the time was still a bit limited. I didn't know what I could do. I was vacillating between "I want to do it" and "I don't know if I can do it."

My mom was dedicated to helping me achieve my aim of learning. I'd learn thirty words a day, and her role was to ask me the definitions of these new words. Each day, I'd give her a list, and she'd ask me what they meant, and I had to pronounce them properly and explain them to her. It was amazing to me to feel that I could speak, read, and communicate. I kept living in the dictionary. I woke up and went to bed with it. It taught me how to read words and build sentences. I was also grateful that my mom took the time to ask me and to listen, so I could train and memorize the words. I fell in love with reading. It was one of the most amazing things.

As I studied and read more, I could answer more and more questions people asked, so little by little I was gaining confidence. The higher the value of something is for you, the more focus and organization you want to put into it. At that time, my highest value was learning to read and learning the laws of the universe – period. I was learning how to read, and I was getting faster and faster at it. I started developing my own speed-reading techniques, like mnemonics and shorthand systems. Every night I asked two questions – what had worked and what hadn't worked that day in relation to my reading. Every night I just kept asking the same two questions. I started compiling what worked. I found certain things that helped my reading over and over again. One of them was making sure I linked whatever I was reading to my goals and dreams of being a great master teacher, healer and philosopher. I wanted to understand the evolution of human consciousness, and I wanted to expand my mind and to become more aware of the natural laws governing the universe. So, whatever I read, I would link the new material to how it would help in the evolution of human consciousness. I also noticed the effect that gratitude had on my learning – that's right, the Gratitude Effect. If I was grateful, I remembered everything that I had learnt that night. If I was in a state of gratitude, I had a much better retention of material and showed greater mental capacities.

These ongoing daily discoveries eventually allowed me to develop a supersonic speed-reading rate. One day, after many years of developing my reading skills, I was able to read eleven thousand pages. As I was devouring all these texts, I noticed something quite profound. Even when I didn't know for sure if I had remembered what I had just read at the moment, days later, weeks later, or months later, I would be speaking, possibly in one of my nightly classes or at some conference, and out would come that information. I didn't even know I had that in me, but it surfaced when I least expected it and when I needed it. It gave me more confidence to realize that whatever I was reading was all going in and somehow staying. Nothing was lost. When I really needed it, it was there.

I quit questioning my mind's ability. I became grateful for all the knowledge that would thereafter remain in my mind, and whenever I needed it, it would be there. It became my new affirmation, "I am a master reader. I have a photographic and audio-graphic mind, and whatever I read, I retain." This made a difference. I was able to excel because of this. But it all started with linking things to my ever evolving mission, my highest values, my most inspiring dreams, and being grateful for the opportunity to read. When I read my first book and put it down, I felt really grateful for this opportunity. Now I've read over twenty-eight thousand and five hundred books, but every time I pick up a book, I'm still grateful for the opportunity to read. And now because of awakening this skill, I am able to share with people throughout the world the power of the written word along with – the Gratitude Effect.

Man stands in his own shadow and wonders why it's dark.
– ZEN SAYING

What Happens When We Don't Listen to Our Intuition

The intuitive mind is a sacred gift and the rational mind is a faithful servant. We have created a society that honors the servant and has forgotten the gift.
– ALBERT EINSTEIN

After beginning my journey of learning how to read, I was soon introduced by my parents to a special collection of books, written by Norman Vincent Peal, about the power of positive thinking. After finally devouring this set of books, I began attempting to become only positive. Since then I've probably read every book on positive thinking available in English, and attended dozens of positive thinking seminars and rallies.

All that time my inner voice was whispering to me, "But you are not always positive." There was a part of me that didn't want to admit that I also had what appeared to be a negative side. I was putting on a positive mask, a façade, half of the time, trying to hide the other so-called negative counterpart. I didn't want anyone to know about my illusive negative side once I was informed that I was only to be positive. Guess, what happened. My other so-called "negative" part kept showing up in my private life. When I didn't feel well or was in a bad mood, I wanted to be alone, away from everyone, I had to isolate it and keep it all to myself and to... that's right, the people I loved the most. Then I noticed that the more I tried to put on a positive façade in my public life, the more negative my private life was becoming. The people who weren't so important to me were getting most or all my positive pole, while my closest loved ones and I would catch all the negativity. Clearly, this wasn't working for me. It seemed that the more I tried to become only one sided, the more I punished myself and those close to me.

I wondered what was wrong with me, and why I couldn't be positive all the time. I was feeling pseudo-gratitude when I felt I was only positive. At the same time, I was pseudo-ungrateful for the other half of myself and was beating myself up when I wasn't living up to this one-sided fantasy. This whole time, my intuition was telling me, "There's something missing in the picture. This can't be it. It doesn't have to be so much of a struggle to be a human being. Why are you trying to get rid of half of your life?"

Then I thought, maybe someone else figured it out. So, I went and interacted with various self-help gurus and positive thinking teachers (we are talking about top people in the positive thinking field). I went to their seminars, met them, spoke to them, and found out, one by one, that all of them had both polarities. Not one of them was all positive all the time.

And I was actually able to observe them first hand in moments of extreme negativity. It was a liberating experience.

Simply seeing to complete the picture wasn't good enough for me. I had to be sure. That's when I decided to do my own little analysis. Over the period of two years, four times a day, every day, I was documenting my moods in all seven areas of my life – spiritual, mental, vocational, financial, familial, social and physical – collecting hard evidence on whether I was more up or more down in each area. I used a scale from -3 to +3, and found out that I was not more up than I was down. I was perfectly balanced. It wasn't even fifty-one to forty-nine per cent one way or the other; it was fifty-fifty. That's when I concluded, "I can't be one-sided, even though I am diligently focused on it, studying it, learning it, going to seminars, reading books, buying CDs, doing everything that a human being can do to succeed at it. If I can't do it, then, the people I'm teaching probably aren't going to do it either. I just can't teach it anymore. I can't teach a one-sided state. I have not obtained it. It must be an incomplete concept. It's a lie." And I didn't want to be up there telling a lie.

Men occasionally stumble over the truth, but most of them pick themselves up and hurry off as if nothing ever happened.
– *SIR WINSTON CHURCHILL*

Long before I did my little experimental self-analysis, before I figured it out intellectually, my intuition had already inwardly known the truth. It was trying to tell me that there were two sides to my nature, and that my search for one-sidedness was incomplete and would only result in futility. I finally looked at myself differently, and, as a result, owned and embraced both sides of myself. That was one of the most liberating moments of my life. It was scary because I wasn't sure how my new realization and ultimate message would be received by others.

I was anxious about what my colleagues would think of me when I said that we were not designed to be positive all the time. I stood before the group and told them that I wasn't going to teach them how to be only one sided, that is, happy without sad or successful without failure or even nice without mean, seventy-five people got up and walked out on me.

I remember the moment when people started getting up and leaving. That was not the easiest moment of my life, but there was nothing I knew that could change that. So I just spoke from my heart and said, "If you need to walk out, I understand, but I can't tell you what I personally do not believe in any more". The people who stayed there, listened to my newly found truth, and I rebuilt a new audience. It was a scary day, but once I got over that, it was done. I had to go through that because I just knew it was true. It was this analysis and personal breakthrough, together with many years of client research and thousands of demonstrations of this principle that catapulted me forward to share with even greater numbers – the Gratitude Effect. And it is the Gratitude Effect that emerges when we embrace the truth of this balance along with its magnificent wholeness.

Almost every area of research and nearly every discipline demonstrate and teach this beautiful balance of opposites, except the following three "-ologies": psychology, sociology and theology. Here lay perpetuated fantasies imposed on human beings that make them think they can be one-sided. Few other disciplines have such polarized illusions. This desire for one-sidedness will not stand a chance in other disciplines, such as, physics because every atom has a positive and a negative part. In geology we learn that Earth itself has a positive and a negative pole. Nothing in the universe can be one-sided except in the fantasy of human minds. This illusion permeates those three "-ologies", and I think it is time to revamp them and bring them into alignment with the natural laws of the universe.

In the world, I see both peace and war, cooperation and

competition, support and challenge, friends and enemies. Have you ever seen one side only? If you had ever truly eliminated your so-called negative side, would you have made it to where you are today? The key to initiating the Gratitude Effect is the full embrace of both sides of your existence which are actually making up your one true whole. You are worthy of love for both halves of your complete nature.

There are many other cultural and religious philosophies like Taoism and Buddhism that, at least partly, teach such a wholesome balance. Apparently, initially I had been introduced to and believed in an incomplete philosophical teaching that I later had the opportunity to transcend. I was scared initially by the transition, but I did it. And I am very grateful that I did because it was a major breakthrough for me. I realized that the mono-polar fantasies that we so often unwisely strive for are the source of their accompanying mono-polar nightmares or our so-called depressions. Our very negative thoughts emerge as a result of our unrealistic expectations. The Buddhists say that the desire for that which is unobtainable is the source of human suffering. Albert Einstein said that religious idealisms are often the source of human suffering, and of course both theories are wise for ultimately recognizing this and other great laws. So this deeper realization is what finally helped me decide to teach the wholesomeness of complete and synchronous balance. And my physiology, my intuition and my environment had all been guiding me to that realization. Isn't it true that if and when we become proud, we get humbled, and if we get down, we get supported? Our intuition is trying to do everything it can to awaken us to this divine and soulful perfection and balance. And the second we awaken to it, we innately feel poise and gratitude.

The universe has laws that govern it, and these very laws are believed by some to imply a great universal intelligence. And maybe this grand organizing principle is guiding us to grow and evolve through our appreciation for life. May we all be wise and learn to deeply listen to this subtle and yet grand universal guidance, and may we all share with others – the Gratitude Effect!

If we could understand the order of the universe well enough, we would find that it surpasses all the wishes of the wisest, and that it's impossible to make it better than it is.
– *LEIBNIZ*

The universe already has magnificence. It's inherent in the grandly organized system. What we are often trying to do is to build a fantasy of how it's supposed to be, and we torture ourselves because it does not match our fantasy. That's our hell. I think hell is our own creation based on our unrealistic expectations that are not met. When we are ungrateful, we experience what some theologians call hell. And when we are grateful, we have our inner state of heaven. When Pope John Paul II was asked what heaven was, he said – gratitude.

Many people become addicted to one-sided delusions or fantasies, which become their inner sources of opium. Once they become addicted, they can then begin to experience the inevitable withdrawal symptoms that accompany these delusions when they become unobtainable. That's one of the reasons why some cultures become so drug dependent. They want pleasure without pain, happiness without sadness, niceness without meanness, etc. And you can become conditioned to think that if you are not that way, something must be wrong with you. But let me tell you right now that nothing is wrong with you. You are perfect just the way you are – with your perfect balance of opposites. So embrace yourself, release your illusive addiction, and let yourself become master of the Gratitude Effect.

But I Am Not Worthy

You have to believe in yourself, that's the secret. Even when I was in the orphanage, when I was roaming the street trying to find enough to eat, even then I thought of myself as the greatest actor in the world. I had to feel the exuberance that comes from utter confidence in yourself. Without it, you go down to defeat.

– *CHARLIE CHAPLIN*

There are at least three states that any human being can be in. We can put ourselves down, beat ourselves up, minimize ourselves, and self-deprecate. On the other hand, we can build ourselves up with pride and think that we are greater and better than others. I love the third state. We can be balanced and see that everyone is a reflection of us. Then we don't put ourselves above or below others. I find that every time we feel shy or unworthy, we have another area in our life where we are being cocky and proud. Maybe I can say this better with a story.

A short time ago, a nice lady brought her teenage son for a consultation with me and said that he had problems with his school grades, was shy because his face was covered with pimples, had so-called low self-esteem, and was therefore constantly beating himself up.

The first question I asked him was: "So, where do you think you are better, greater, and smarter than most kids?"

First he hesitated, then looked at his mom and finally said, "In skateboarding. I can do things on my skateboard no one else can."

So, it's not that he was lacking confidence in general. He was very confident in the area that was really important to him, which was skateboarding, and he knew he was the best there. But he was being an introvert in the area that was not important to him, which happened to be school. His mother and other well-meaning people were projecting their values onto him saying that his grades should be important. He was simply not buying this.

I asked, "Do you think school is boring, and is that why you are not excelling there?"

"Yeah, they are always on my case there."

I said, "Imagine, if you were in a school that specialized in skateboarding. Would you be the leading student there?"

"Absolutely."

"Well, unfortunately, I don't know of a school like that, but until you can connect how going to a regular school can help you succeed at skateboarding, you are probably going to be bored and you are not going to put your full energy into it."

"But I can't see how it's gonna help me. It's just all boring stuff."

I had to help him link those things that his parents wanted from him to how it was going to help him with what he loved doing – skateboarding. That changed his perception and eventually, his so-called self-esteem in school.

We have confidence in the areas that truly matter most to us, and little or zero confidence in things we don't care about. Nobody escapes that. One gives you confidence – the other humbles you and teaches you how to learn. The key is to move your career and your life in the direction of your confidence or highest values so that you will be doing something that inspires you. Otherwise, you will be feeling so-called low self-esteem because you are going against your values.

Resolve to be thyself: and know, that he who finds himself, loses his misery.
– *MATTHEW ARNOLD*

Your confidence lives in the area that is at the top of your values list. That's where you have order and certainty. If you don't feel confident, it's probably because you have tried to inject someone else's values into your life, or you are expecting yourself to have confidence in the area that's really not important to you.

Recently, I happened to be at a large computer conference at the Jarvis Center in New York. Computer technology is one of those areas I have little knowledge about. I know how to type a book, but that's about it. So I felt like a real gimp there. All these intelligent geeks were presenting their ingenious devices; they were way ahead of me. In fact, I felt like I was still in the Dark Ages. When I went to talk to two people there, I was unusually quiet, like an introvert. You could tell by their faces that they thought that I was an idiot. The truth is, I excel in my area of expertise, but I am meek and humble in theirs. I don't have confidence there because it hasn't been important to me – it has not been on the top of my values list. When I am in a group of people who specialize in computers, I look uncertain, insecure, awkward and uncomfortable. It serves a purpose too. It allows me to learn to listen. It allows me to humble myself and appreciate other people in the world and learn from them. Both confidence and doubt serve a purpose, and we don't need to get rid of any part of ourselves in order to love ourselves. Every part serves us, and there is nothing to get rid of.

The greatest of news is that you don't have to be stuck with your present values either. There are ways to change them if you choose to. Let's say that computers and schoolwork are really low on your hierarchy of values, and skateboarding and sports are the highest ones. The key is to link the lower priorities to the higher ones. Ask yourself how doing the low priority stuff will help you excel in what matters to you most. If you can't see the connection, you will certainly never excel at it because you simply won't excel at something you are not interested in. But the second you see a connection between your highest goals and what you don't like doing, you will change your attitude and will be inspired to do it. The way to bump something up on your value list is to stack up the benefits of doing it and write down how it will serve your highest objectives in life. When I say stack up, I am not talking about five or ten benefits, I'm talking hundreds. Then you will get a light-bulb moment of "Oh my God, I can achieve my goals by doing this." Then your self-worth in this area is guaranteed to grow. That is something to be grateful for.

With gratitude your mind becomes the best place around to spend your time.
– *DR JOHN DEMARTINI*

How wonderful it is to have a mind of our own; a mind that can ponder the mysteries of life, sort through everyday priorities, file information for future reference, assist us in learning new skills, set standards, form relationships, have opinions, and then give us an option to choose to change our minds and alter those opinions. Our minds make up our private world, the secret part of ourselves that often remains a mystery to others, but becomes an intimate friend or foe to us, depending on how we master our mind's perceptions, or how our unsettling perceptions run us. Most of us take for granted the diverse and marvellous powers of our mind and its many rich gifts. The Gratitude Effect will help your mind to grow and expand beyond any limitations imposed by your present beliefs.

Any time I experience a tear of gratitude, I document it. I find that it's a special moment when my mind is most aligned to my highest values or purpose. My tears of gratitude are a feedback from my body to my mind, saying that I am on track and am doing what I am meant to do. I let my tears of inspiration be my guide. Our intuition is guiding us to what inspires us. When we exaggerate ourselves, we have a part of us that whispers, "Who, do you think, you are?" When we minimize ourselves, it goes, "I know, I can do better than that." Our intuition is at work, trying hard to get us to be centred and balanced and most importantly, authentic and inwardly grateful. When we are, our mind is inspired and we are surprised by our own genius. That is the Gratitude Effect for you.

Questions to Help you Discover Your Genius

- What did I learn today that I can be grateful for?
- What is my intuition revealing to me today?
- What is my disowned part whispering to my owned part?
- What area would I love to explore, and how would this exploration be fulfilling in my life?
- How can I master my learning today, and how will that help me?
- What strategies have I uncovered today that can enhance my mastery of life and learning?

Affirmations to Help You Realize Your Genius

- Thank you, intuition, for guiding me to what's really inspiring to me.
- Thank you for the opportunity to be exposed to this refining challenge today.
- Thank you for the people in my life who have brought to me their own opinions that expanded my own.
- Thank you for the insight that has been revealed to me by my intuition or by others.
- I am a genius, and I apply my wisdom.
- I have a masterful mind. It directs me wisely, it inspires me, and I am thankful.
- I am an incredible soul, I have an incredible mind, and ingenious ideas come to me daily.

- I am present, and my mind is clear, sharp and focused.
- I listen to the voice of my soul and obey promptly.
- When I experience events without judgement, I show wisdom.
- I am wise; for, I instantaneously recognize that crises are blessings.
- My innermost dominant thoughts become my outermost tangible reality.
- I understand anything I set my mind to.
- I focus on the flowers, not the weeds.
- I see my dreams so clearly in my mind that they simply manifest.
- I soar far above and beyond the average, for my vision is extraordinarily clear.

Take the First Step

The fastest way to learn something is to share it with someone. Find someone with whom you can share your most inspiring idea, or discovery you've made today. Before going to bed, either write an email, get on a telephone, or communicate with someone directly what was most inspiring to you today so as to help inspire others. If you help others inspire their lives, it helps you inspire yours.

CHAPTER 4

Doing What You Love and Loving What You Do

Work is love made visible. And if you cannot work with love but only with distaste, it is better that you should leave your work and sit at the gate of the temple and take alms of those who work with joy.

– KAHLIL GIBRAN

Are you Ready for the Balance?

You may be using your genius and serving others by running your own business. There are two true business gems I would like to share with you that may save you a lot of frustration. For every so-called over-worker in your company, there will be at least one under-worker, and for every outspoken person, there will be someone or some many who are hiding what they truly want to say to others deep inside. In other words, there will always be a complementarity of opposites. When we can appreciate this grand universal principle, we can begin to manage our business relations more effectively. As long as we are infatuated with someone in our company, we will also be resentful of that person's opposite. When we can embrace both of them equally and simultaneously and see that they are just trying to hone us in on a central standard point – that jumps up to a new higher standard the moment the pair of opposites is recognized and truly appreciated – then we will feel competent and grateful. When we understand the necessity of both poles and we feel gratitude for them equally, we get to grow our business. This will non-locally impact and transform that pair of working opposites and allow the Gratitude Effect to create its magic.

What Language are You Speaking?

It takes a great man to be a good listener.
– *CALVIN COOLIDGE*

Any time we care enough about our colleagues or customers to communicate in the language of their values, we open the doorway for effective communication and fair exchange, and they will, no doubt, appreciate us for doing that. This is one of the key things in building a growing and fulfilling business. You are taking something that inspires you, a product, service, or idea that you want to share with the world, and you are finding people who have a void they want to fill. You are trying to link what you have to offer with how it will fulfill their needs. If you are able to do this artfully, they would feel that they are getting what they want, and you would feel that you are getting what you want. It's a fair exchange. But if people feel that you are projecting on them what you think they need, but it's not what they really need; or if they are expecting you to give them something that you don't have or don't want to give, you've got miscommunication. In this case, business usually plateaus or even begins to crumble.

If we do not appreciate our jobs, promotions would not come our way easily. If we do not appreciate the products, services, or ideas we provide, why would someone want to buy them from us? If we do not appreciate the people we work with, why would we enjoy our time at work? And if we do not appreciate the cause or vision of the company we work for, why would that company go very far? None of these are "win-win" situations. None of these scenarios can take advantage of the Gratitude Effect.

Peter Lynch, a successful Wall Street stock investor whose record ranks him as one of the greatest stock-pickers in the world, once believed that, when selecting companies to invest in, it is wise to look for those that are filled with people who appreciate their careers, their clients, and their products. If people aren't appreciative and are not inspired to go to work then it is riskier to invest in the company they work for. That's one of the more important things in investment diagnostics. The company will more likely appreciate in value in the stock market if people working for it arc filled with appreciation.

Every product has certain energy associated with it. If that product is not produced with love and appreciation, you can feel it. Imagine, you go to a restaurant, and the chef doesn't have appreciation for the food he is preparing. He doesn't like cooking. In fact, he wants to be an architect, and, while cooking, he is dreaming about going back to school and studying architecture. His mind is somewhere else. I bet you will be able to taste it. But if the moment you get your food, the chef comes out and asks you, "What do you think?" If he was inspired to create the food, it becomes a real masterpiece, and you can taste his loving energy in it. He literally channels his loving divine inspiration into the food that now tastes divine.

God gave you a gift of 86,400 seconds today.
Have you used one to say "thank you"?
– *WILLIAM A. WARD*

Appreciation comes through as a vibration in every aspect of a company, from the top to the bottom, and makes the company either soar or become a sore. In business, gratitude is the key for survival. If there is no gratitude in the company, there's no soul in it. Put simply, it is declining or dying.

I once had the opportunity to consult with the head of a major wood and paper company. He was feeling burned out in his position. He just wanted to endure a couple more years so that he could retire. He wasn't feeling grateful for his work anymore and lost his inspiration somewhere along the way. When I met him, his only goal was to make sure he got enough money to retire. His foreign competitors were getting stronger. He felt that there was no way to compete in the North American and Asian markets. First, he became overwhelmed and then just angry at the market because he felt unappreciated by it. He wasn't appreciative of his staff, and all he could see was that they were costing his company.

The people who called me to arrange the consultation were technically his employees. They felt that he was interfering with the success of the company. They couldn't get rid of him because he was the owner, but, at the same time, they wanted to get the company going again. They asked me to consult with him so that he could get his vision back. We spent the whole day working on that objective. I told him that just because his competitor was taking over the market didn't mean that we couldn't create a new legend, a new story, a new marketing plan, and have people inspired by it and have the market run with it. I asked him, "Do you remember why you began working in this industry? Why did you do it? What inspired you?"

I asked him to fill out the Demartini Method® form to clear

him of all his past and present emotionally charged baggage concerning his company. He finally broke through and once again saw clearly what he was there for, and what his mission was. He remembered that when he was growing up, his parents didn't have a lot of money. Paper was special, and there wasn't a whole lot of it. Well, at least, in his family. Finally, one day, his parents brought home a big ream of paper, and for the first time he could draw freely. That was a very special day for him. It was so inspiring to him that he decided that later, when he was an adult, he would make sure everyone in the world had enough paper.

When he rediscovered his lost childhood mission, this sixty-year-old man broke down in tears. What occurred to him as a kid had profoundly influenced his life, and he remembered it. He reconnected with his childhood dream of having enough paper to draw. He got in touch with his main purpose of why he was selling paper to the people.

I asked him, "Are you going to let this temporary illusion and perception of setback stop you from fulfilling your childhood mission? Paper makes the world go around. Tell me, who can sell paper better than a person who had a childhood dream of bringing paper into the world? You can't let anything stop you from your mission."

He cleared his eyes, cleared his throat and said, "You are right. I have been buying into this idea that I should retire by a certain age. I started winding down, but that's not what I really want to do. It is not my true dream."

I told him, "Let's get back on track with what's true. Let's create a story about kids, market it, have people inspired by your story, and create a new campaign for your product. Let's create an image of a nationally unique product and make people be proud for their country when they buy it." And we did. We did all of that. We turned his company around just in the matter of months. He reclaimed his vision and became grateful and inspired about what he was doing once again. The Gratitude Effect revitalized his company. I bet, it also added five or ten years to his life.

How to Learn to Love a Job You Hate in Ten Minutes

Find a job you like and you add five days to every week.
– *H. JACKSON BROWN, JR*

The Gratitude Effect in the business world stems from being grateful for what you are doing, for the vision of doing it, for the people who are doing it with you, for the people who are buying your product or service, and for looking forward to getting up in the morning to do what you love doing. This is how I feel every morning. Every day, I get up to research, write, travel, and speak. Those are the four things I love doing the most. I am certainly grateful for this opportunity. If you aren't grateful for what you do, you hold yourself back. And it means you just haven't asked yourself the right questions or haven't taken the action steps towards the fulfillment of your dreams. It is not about "once I get there, I'll be grateful". It is about being grateful for every step you take along the way.

If people go to work and can't see how it is going to help them fulfill their top goals and live according to their highest values, there is no way they are going to be fully grateful for their work. They are going to want more money, more outside motivation, more incentives, more time off, take more breaks, and longer vacations. Eventually it is going to cost the company more. One of the more important goals of the company is to communicate its mission to its employees in such a way that they can see that it is aligned to their highest values and that it helps them fulfill their own objectives. This way the company is grateful for the employees, and they, in turn, are grateful for the opportunity to work there.

I don't know of anyone who doesn't want to work and learn new things that are important to them. That's our nature. But when we have to do something we don't love doing or we have to learn something we don't want to learn, it is discouraging and unfulfilling. The way to turn such an unfulfilling scenario around is to learn to ask quality questions. Here is couple of examples. "How is what I'm doing going to help me fulfill my mission? What would I love to do? How can I get handsomely paid to do it? What are the seven high priority action steps that can help me achieve my goals and that I can take today?" But don't stop at asking. Take the first step. Suddenly, you will find yourself doing what you love. When your vocation and your vacation are the same, you have begun to master your life. People ask me what I do on vacation. I research, write, travel, and speak. Surprise! This is both my vocation and my vacation. This is my life, and I don't need a vacation from it.

I have designed a form I call the Demartini Productivity Motivation and Loyalty Form that I constantly use in companies while consulting. The form contains a series of questions I ask company employees. In short, I ask them to write down their job description and define everything they do in great detail. Then I ask them to write down a list of their values or what's most meaningful in their life. Then they have to go down the list, item by item, and link each and every one of their job tasks to their highest values and goals. They have to write down how what they are doing will help them realize their goals. If they can't see it, they are not going to be fulfilled in their job. I keep asking them questions until they see it. They have to answer the question differently twenty to thirty times at least until they truly see a lot of connections. When they are finished, all of a sudden they are grateful for the job. And when they are, their productivity, their motivation, their company "loyalty", and their inspiration all go up. They get more out of their career, and companies get more out of their employees.

This inspiring exercise is worth doing even if you think you don't presently know what you are going to do with your future career. If you don't yet know what you'd love to do or don't have the strategy to do it, or if you do know but are frightened to do it, it's insane not to appreciate what you are doing now. It works wonders if you keep doing this exercise until you get a clear perspective. Doing this exercise will allow you to have more vitality and energy in your life. Otherwise, you may just end up fighting yourself all day. You may also be weighing down the company that you work for. And for that matter you may be holding your life back and not helping your health either. It's not what you do – it's how you perceive it. And when you perceive enough benefits to balance out all the drawbacks, and you see how it's going to help you fulfill your purpose in life, suddenly you are grateful and you love what you do. And if later you decide to do something else, that's fine too. You build a plan, and you move towards that, but in the meantime, appreciate what work opportunity you do have. The Gratitude Effect works wonders whether you are already doing what you love or just learning to love what you do. This next story better illustrates what I have just said.

How Gratitude Got Me my First Promotion

Give thanks for a little and you will find a lot.
– A HAUSA (NIGERIA) SAYING

I was not quite sixteen when I was invited by someone from California whom I had met in Hawaii. He even offered to pay for the trip. So, I went to California for a very short time. I stayed in the garage of one of his friends, but I had to get a short-term job to make a little bit of money while I was there.

One has to be sixteen to get a job. So, I lied about my age and got a job at Posa Fuel Carburetor Company which was a branch of Excel Tool and Die Company. I was a machinist and I helped make carburetors for motorcycles. It was basically your minimum wage kind of job. It was dirty too. I had oil and grease all over me the whole day, but I felt so lucky to have gotten a job while underage that every day I would say, "Thank you so much for the job. I truly appreciate it."

The other workers and supervisor could never understand why I would say that. They had never seen a kid who was so grateful for this kind of job. I was just a regular summer hire. Long story short, it was the end of summer, and I was finishing my term and getting ready to go back to my surfing life in Hawaii. The manager of the shop came to me and said, "We were wondering if you would like to continue working here. We want to promote you." I knew I was going back to surfing because that was my dream, so I thanked him and said I couldn't stay.

I really believe this promotion was offered to me because I was so thankful for the job. I was working hard and didn't want to lose that job because I was making $2.75 per hour. And on top of that, I would thank them for my job every day. I think that even if they had known my age, they would have kept me there. When we are grateful for our job, our job becomes easier, we become more efficient, and we get new opportunities for promotions. The Gratitude Effect is really a simple secret of how to live a fulfilling life. People notice the energy of gratitude radiating from you. It is invisible, and yet the results it creates are very real.

Have you Found Your Inner Carpenter Yet?

Whatever you can do or dream you can, begin it.
Boldness has genius, power and magic in it. Begin it now.
– *JOHANN VON GOETHE*

I would love to tell you this story about the importance of following your heart and encouraging others to do what they love. At one point, I needed to hire a manager for my business. I was in my office doing the interviews when this gentleman with a briefcase comes in. He looks very confident and enthusiastic. He puts his briefcase down, sits down, leans forward and says assertively, "Dr. Demartini, I just want to let you know that I'm the man for this job."

I go, "Oh, Great! I hope, you don' mind, but I have a couple of questions for you. If I gave you five million dollars, what would you do with your life?"

He was not expecting that. It took him a second to gather his thoughts, and he said, "Well, if I had five million dollars and I didn't have to work anymore, I'd make furniture. I love building furniture with my own hands."

And I said, "Thank you. That will be all."

I stood up and shook his hand. He looked puzzled.

"Are we done with the interview? Have you decided that quickly?"

I said, "Yes sir. You are not the person for the job."

"But I know I can help you with your business... I know I can manage things well... How did you make your decision with one question like that?"

I said, "It's very simple. If you are such a great manager, how is it that you haven't managed your life to be able to do what you love doing? If you love making furniture, how come you haven't made it your career? And if you can't manage your life, how do you expect me to let you manage my company?"

He stared at me for a moment and said, "Wow. That's a powerful question. You got me. I guess I understand that I am not the person for the job."

He thanked me and left. A few weeks later, I was busy with a patient when my assistant came in and said, "There's a gentleman who was here a couple of weeks ago. He is wondering if he can speak with you for a minute."

He came in with a brown paper sack, sat down in the same chair, and said, "Dr. Demartini, I just want to thank you for our meeting a few weeks ago. You asked me the most amazing question. That question has changed my life."

I say, "Tell me what happened."

"Well, I was certain I was going to get the job of being a manager in your company, but your question kind of slammed me. It made me stop and think. I had been looking for a new job for a few months, and that moment in your office was a turning point. I asked myself, 'why can't I go out and make a living doing what I love doing? I've been without a job for about three months anyways, so what have I got to lose?' And I decided to give it a shot. I decided to open a furniture manufacturing company and to make furniture with my own hands. I got inspired. It's as if I got a new life. For the first time in a long while, I was enthused about my life, I felt alive, and I've already acquired new business clients. I'm making furniture, and I can't even believe it myself. I just can't thank you enough. I hope you don't mind, but last time I was in your office I noticed the woodwork in your office, the style and the colour of it, and I made you some wooden Kleenex tissue holders that you can put up in all your exam rooms if you'd like. And I will be happy to mount them for you, if you would be kind enough to let me do it. I'd love to do it as a gift to thank you for starting my company."

I said, "Absolutely. I am glad to see that you are managing your life."

So, he installed wooden Kleenex tissue holders in all the exam rooms and that was the lovely ending of that story. Had I hired him as my manager, he probably wouldn't have been grateful for the job, and I wouldn't have been grateful for him working there. I have a strong suspicion we would both have been unfulfilled. I have learnt that it is wise to hire people who love to do what they are going to do, for it further breeds the Gratitude Effect.

What if I Don't Know My Calling Yet?

Your vision will become clear only when you can look into your own heart. Who looks outside, dreams; who looks inside, awakes.
– *CARL GUSTAV JUNG*

Many people say, "I don't know what I would love to do with my life." But I don't buy into this so-called uncertainty. I simply refuse to believe it. I am convinced that deep down inside all human beings know their heartfelt mission and dreams. They don't admit it because they are living out one or more of the seven fears. They can be afraid of breaking some spiritual or moral authority, or of not being smart enough; or they can be paralysed by the fear of failure, the fear of losing money or family, the fear of rejection, or the fear of ill health and disease, or by all of them piling up on top of each other and silencing the voice of their intuition. As long as those fears are there, people are going to lie to themselves and say, "I don't know what I want." But if those fears were not present, they would be able to declare openly what they would love to do?

They know. You know. Inside us, our soul is always calling us to what we would truly love to do. Gratitude is the key to unlock the fearless living. Because we cannot experience gratitude and fear at the same time, the moment we are in gratitude, we can see past the fears and we can see the possibilities. We are purposeful beings. Our mission and calling is sitting inside our heart and waiting for the Gratitude Effect to open the gate.

It's important to know the difference between pursuing fantasies and pursuing what your life is demonstrating as your heart's desire. Your life is already telling you what is important to you, and there are no mistakes. Everything you have done in your life is pointing you in some direction. Look around. Analyze your life for a moment. What has your life demonstrated about your mission, and what is it directing you to do? If those seven fears were dissolved, what would you love to be, to do, and to have?

Open your heart by thinking about what you are already grateful for in life and then ask yourself the following questions. How do you spend your time? What can you do for hours and not even notice the time passing by? By paying close attention to those moments when you feel inspired, enthused, loving and grateful, you can discover your calling and unveil dreams that are most dear to your heart. These four magical feelings are indicators that you are on track with your life mission. When our hearts are open, our minds become unwavering and clear. Without our inwardly guiding hearts, we would constantly be vacillating among multitude of options and living with a host of uncertainties. The key is listening to the one true inner voice that speaks through our heart.

Once you can hear the message clearly, don't underestimate the power of writing it down. I don't know about anyone else, I can only speak for myself, but I have a book full of very specific objectives related to how exactly I want my life to be, and they come true. I get very clear and specific, but yet flexible and adaptable enough to refine my objectives if something more inspiring and empowering comes along. And I take the time to plan my life. I literally take hours on end to focus on what exactly I want to be, to do, and to have.

I write what I believe my heart is saying, refine it and read it every day. When we keep refining what we have written until we are clear and certain, no matter how long it takes, self-mastery and self-refinement are ours. And the final step to uncovering your heart's desire is a silent passive meditation backed by an active prayer of gratitude for what is, as it is, which I go into every day and wait until some detail is revealed. Once it is clear, I act and then watch the Gratitude Effect do its magic.

How to Transform Your Vocation into a Vacation

Far away there in the sunshine are my highest aspirations.
I may not reach them, but I can look up and see their beauty,
believe in them, and try to follow where they lead.
– *LOUISA MAY ALCOTT*

After we have discovered our heart's desire, feeling productive is one of the most inspiring feelings a person can experience. Being productive and fulfilled doesn't have to be limited to a conventional nine to five work role. Whether you are a homemaker, a student, an athlete, or on holiday, it is important to feel that you have been productive throughout any of the day's activities (in whatever form productivity brings fulfillment to you). For example, if you like to fish, your fulfillment may come from being grateful for a day of fishing. For the businessperson it may mean the opportunity to make some deals. For the homemaker, it may mean baking the dinner for the family – but feeling productive and being grateful for your own form of productivity completes the package of your life. Without it, a great deal of fulfillment will be missing from your everyday existence. The Gratitude Effect provides you with a sense of purpose, achievement and satisfaction.

I prefer using the words "fulfillment" and "achievement" rather than the word "success". Why? Success and failure come as a pair. The second we start to think we are successful, we are on our way down. The second we feel we are a failure, we are on our way up. Fulfillment embraces both of them. Everyone I know who has achieved a lot in life, has experienced both feelings. Both are only due to partial perceptions. The temporary feeling of success is just part of the game. Sometimes when we feel successful, we get puffed up and stop doing what we love doing and go off on distractions and low priority things. When we feel like a failure, we can become prompted to go back to the basics and do high priority things. We need both polarized misperceptions to centre us on our authentic selves – where true fulfillment emerges. When we are planning our achievements, we are wise to think **SMART**, which means having **S**pecific **M**easurable goals that are **A**ligned to our values and that are **R**ealistic and **T**imed – **SMART**.

Imagine that the most amazing person in the world is coming to visit you. Would you change anything in your house or in your schedule to prepare for this visit? If not – great, but most people say that they would change at least a few things. Now, for the trick part, "Why don't you treat yourself as if YOU were the most amazing person? Why don't you take the time to plan your life?" I want to live to the fullest and see what is humanly possible. Personally, I want to be able to say at the end of my life, "That was an extraordinary life." I want to say that I lived my life fully. I got everything I could out of the day. I achieved all the things that are imaginable; and I had amazing gratitude for life. I know if I do just that, I am giving permission to other people to do the same, and that inspires me.

How to be Grateful for Distractions, Confusion and Procrastination

> *Gratitude unlocks the fullness of life. It turns what we have into enough, and more. It turns denial into acceptance, chaos into order, confusion into clarity... It turns problems into gifts, failures into success, the unexpected into perfect timing, and mistakes into important events. Gratitude makes sense of our past, brings peace for today and creates a vision for tomorrow.*
>
> – *MELODIE BEATTIE*

The number one question I get asked around the world is "How do I stay focused?" I believe that it is as important to be grateful for focus as it is to be grateful for distractions. I also believe that when one is having a hard time focusing, one is trying to live according to someone else's values. No one has to get me up in the morning to do what I love doing. No one has to get me focused on what I love doing. I love what I am doing. It's my highest value. If I set objectives that are aligned with my highest values, I automatically stay focused. If I pursue objectives that are not aligned with my values, I will constantly feel distracted. This means that I'm at least partly trying to live someone else's life and values and not just my own.

I would love to share a brief story with you about a lovely teenage girl named Veronica. She loves socializing – parties, friends, fun things, and definitely fashion shopping. She loves fashion label shopping because it allows her to be cool in her social circles, and of course lets her feel more beautiful. While her father is inspired by her social and shopping skills, he also loves the idea of her receiving her essential secondary education, so that she knows how to count her money when she is shopping. But the importance of more formal education is certainly an outside value that he has injected into her life as a parent. Because socializing and beauty were highest on her values list, every time she would try to focus on her college classes, she would get distracted by ever emerging social opportunities, parties, and events. She would tell herself, "I know college is important," and go right back to partying. No matter what she tried, she was not staying focused on her more formal education.

Then her mother and father were able to find another local college with a curriculum that enabled her to specialize in fashion and retail. Shopping is second on her list of priorities after socializing. Now that she can see how her personally selected classes are going to help her do what she loves, she likes her classes and is thankful for her specialized learning. Her mind started to awaken to the value of her classes since they were aligned to her higher values. She can more effectively remember what she has learnt, assimilate it easier, apply her knowledge, and share it with others. Once she made a connection between her education and her higher interests, she has been more inspired to go to school and she has less difficulty staying focused because she is finally working toward and achieving what she loves. She was only distracted from school when she couldn't see how her classes were helping her achieve what she wanted. Actually, she was not really distracted – she was just trying to live her values. Now the school is linked to her highest values, and she loves it.

What some people perceive as a distraction may actually be their intuition trying to communicate their highest values to them. So, when you feel distracted, it is wise to be grateful to your intuition for the clue that you are not living your life as you would love to live it. Our so-called distractions may merely be indicators that we are trying to live according to someone else's values. Once we listen carefully and respond wisely we can be grateful for such inner prompting.

The hardest arithmetic to master is that which enables us to count our blessings.
– *ERIC HOFFER*

Confusion is another gift. When you are confused, you are either trying to tackle too many things at the same time or are possibly doing something about which you know very little, something that is not important to you and has no connection to your higher values. You can also be overconfident and cocky thinking you can do it and don't need help when it is wise to ask for mentorship. When I am confused, I ask for help. Just a little while ago, I was confused on what to do with my training programme I had launched all around the world. I had hired facilitators and teachers and had to manage it. All the countries have different laws and rules. I knew I wanted to do it, but I was confused about how exactly to do it. I called a couple of people who had specialized in global training programme development. Some of them had been doing it for over thirty years. I sat down with them, told them about my situation, listened to their expert advice, and delegated some things. They went and hired other professionals and now my global training programme is beginning to thrive. So out of that confusion, I received new social contacts, met people who knew how to do something I didn't,and learnt how to delegate more. That allowed me to focus on what I loved doing. Now I will be able to handle a similar situation in the future. Being confused can be a feedback system too. It is never what happens to you, it is how you interpret it.

People who make decisions clearly and quickly usually accomplish more than those who don't. Taking an immediate action is not as hard as you think. An action may be simply to plan or to really think about something, to get mentorship, or put a strategy together. Getting into action and overcoming inertia is rewarding. There are three things that stop people from taking action. The objective may be unclear, or it may not be chunked into smaller bites, or finally it may not be linked to your highest values. If it's clear, chunked and linked, you'll act. Once you take action steps toward accomplishing your objectives, you increase the probability of shining The Gratitude Effect.

You see things and you say "Why?" but I dream things that never were and I say "Why not?"
– GEORGE BERNARD SHAW

Questions to Help you Love What you do

- How is what I'm doing now going to help me fulfill my mission?
- What would I love to be, to do and to have?

- How can I get handsomely paid to do it?
- What are the seven high priority action steps that can help me achieve my goals?
- What are the seven high priority action steps that I can take today?

If you find yourself having a low day at your current job, you have a lopsided perception of having more negatives than positives. Just ask the following questions to come back to the centre with gratitude:

- Who did I serve today?
- What did I do that worked today?
- What customers did I love helping?

If you are elated about your work on any particular day and need to get back to balance, ask the following questions:

- Who did I forget to serve today?
- What did I do that didn't work today?
- What customers did I not enjoy helping?

Affirmations to Help You Stay on Track

- I am grateful for the opportunity to find my talents and see how they can be expressed.
- I am grateful for the opportunity to be in the position where I have the opportunity to be innovative, creative and expressive.
- I am grateful to be able to make a great living and provide for my family and my loved ones.
- I am grateful for all the people wanting to assist me, as well as people wanting to challenge me.
- I am grateful for the people who create services, products or

ideas that help me fulfill my mission.

- I am grateful that there are needs out there in the world and for the opportunity to contribute to the world and make a difference.
- I have a purpose and I am here to fulfill it.
- I have a mission and I am here to manifest it.
- I have a vision and I am here to empower it.
- I have a message and I am here to share it.
- I have a master plan and I am here to follow it.
- Everything I experience helps me fulfill my purpose.
- I keep growing for I have a purpose bigger than myself.
- I have the power to transform my inspiring ideas into realities.
- I do what I love; and I love what I do.
- I make decisions rapidly and follow them patiently.
- I am at the right place and the right time to meet the right people to make the right deal.
- I assist others in maximizing their talents while I maximize my own.
- I know exactly what I love and I just do it.
- I am a master of persistence, and I do what it takes. I let neither pains nor pleasures interfere with the pursuit of my purpose.
- My purpose is crystal clear and I am on target.
- I am extremely certain that amazing opportunities keep coming to me.
- I prioritize my daily actions and stay on top priority. I act on priorities daily. I follow the A B C s not the X Y Z s.
- My greatest asset is my love of serving, and I am grateful for the opportunity to serve.

Homework

Exercise 1. When I first started my chiropractic healing practice, I used to thank each patient on a nightly basis. Every night, after finishing with my last patient of the day, I filled out a little gratitude form (see a sample below). As I got more patients, it got more challenging, but I kept doing it every night. I just wrote a one-line thank you for each patient. Try it for yourself and enjoy watching the Gratitude Effect in action. What you think about and thank about, you bring about.

Customer Focus Thankfulness Form		Date:_______
Customer Name	Customer Lesson	Customer Blessing to be Grateful For

Exercise 2. Upon arising in the morning, set yourself seven highest priority action steps you commit to taking that day that will ensure productivity. Do these actions first before any less-productive distractions occur – and if you follow this seven highest action steps daily rule, you are certain to finish each day of the week with a sense of gratitude for what you have achieved. (Not to mention that your life is likely to make a quantum leap forward economically as well).

Exercise 3. Make a list of every single person, including your suppliers, lawyers, customers, bankers, who impacts your business, and who you can be grateful for. They all are working for you. This list should also include your competitors who are pushing you to grow and keep you on the edge so that you don't get stagnant, and the government that challenges you and keeps you creative and innovative. All of them are all part of the divine perfection – all reminders of the Gratitude Effect.

CHAPTER 5

How to Build Wealth with the Power of Gratitude

Wealth is the product of man's capacity to think.
– AYN RAND

Being grateful for one's financial situation can be challenging at times. But we must master the "attitude of gratitude" for true wealth to be ours. For most people, managing their finances becomes a source of constant concern and pressure. There are few who can truthfully say that they are consistently grateful for their ongoing financial situations. The more grateful they are though, the faster they tune into the forces that attract greater financial abundance. So many people are in the habit of constantly telling themselves that they don't have enough money. This very attitude of "I don't have enough money" can become a self-defeating prophecy and make their lives seemingly miserable. They often miss the many riches that surround them because they are too busy worrying or feeling "less wealthy" than others.

On the other hand, some people are born with what seems to be a silver spoon in their mouth and feel that they have hardly done anything to earn the money they have. Because their income seems to be easy money, it sometimes has less meaning for them. They may have even shown ingratitude while receiving it. But, if we don't appreciate the wealth that we have received already, we are more likely to miss out on the fulfillment of life it can bring. Our "life" is directly proportional to how much gratitude we have. If we don't appreciate our life, if we don't appreciate what we have, it becomes less meaningful to us and can simply become clutter. To transcend this feeling, begin making an ongoing list of all the things you can be grateful for: things that you already have, such as, money and other assets, and opportunities to produce more, so that you receive more. The Gratitude Effect can bring abundance as well as more overall life.

Look and you will find it – what is unsought will go undetected.
– SOPHOCLES

Everyone has wealth. If you think you don't, you just haven't recognized it yet because it's in a form that eludes you. Your wealth can be in the form of your children, your friends, your business, your spirituality, your body, or anything really. It will take the form of whatever is highest on your hierarchy of values. If your highest value is your children, your wealth and your investment will be in the form of your children. When you are sixty, seventy or eighty, and you are retired, they will probably be taking care of you. Your investment will thus come back to you with its many rewards. If your highest value is your religion and your church, the church may provide for you when you get older. Once again, your investment will pay off. If you place the highest value on your physical body, then you may live long and healthy, and your body may be what supports you. If your highest value is money, your financial investments will most likely be the form of wealth that takes care of you in the future. If your highest value is your friends and your social circle, then your friends will probably take care of you when you are unable to do it yourself anymore.

If you take one thing from this chapter, let it be the knowledge that that you are not missing wealth. You already have something you can be grateful for. But if you would love your wealth to be in the form of cash, you have to appreciate that form of wealth. You have to put it higher on your values list, or cash is not going to show up in your life. The word wealth has more to do with well being than with money. Everyone has wealth and abundance, but it may be manifested in a different form for everyone. If, however, you would like to have it in the form of dollars, then read on.

It has been my observation that people who appreciate the value of money and the opportunity to "receive and give" money are the people who end up creating great financial wealth. I have also worked with people who have very little financial wealth, and they usually say, "Well, I'm really not in it for the money. Money is not important to me. That is not why I do what I do. If I make some money, it would be great but if I don't, I'll do whatever job is available anyway."

The people who have financial wealth usually have a cause for it – they have the know-how to manage it, and want to do something amazing with it. Personal financial freedom is not their sole purpose. They have a cause that is greater than themselves. They have a vision of service they can provide for their community, their country, or even the entire planet. They appreciate and value money. They study it and put focused energy into creating it. They know that they are responsible for what they do with money, and they love this responsibility.

Bill Gates became a billionaire because he found a product that almost everyone on the planet uses. I have developed the Demartini Method®, a tool that I know everyone can benefit from. You too have inside you something that can be of service to everyone in the world. Look for it. You just need to get it out there, and you are a potential billionaire.

I'm Gonna Tell You a Secret, but You Can't Tell Anyone

Whoever appreciates, receives.
– DR JOHN DEMARTINI

Gratitude is the most important tool for wealth building that I know of. There are two main principles of wealth building. First, you have to appreciate yourself. Second, you have to appreciate wealth. Money automatically flows to whoever values it most.

Money is just like people. It wants to be loved and appreciated. If you don't appreciate people, they go somewhere else. If you don't appreciate money, it goes somewhere where it's appreciated more. To show our appreciation for it, we can study it, learn about it, focus on it, and master it. I ask people by a thousand, "How many of you want to be wealthy?" They all put their hands up. Then I ask, "How many of you are wealthy?" This time I usually see very few hands. That's because money is very low on their values list. The hierarchy of our values dictates our financial destiny.

If you buy a piece of property, and the market goes up, your property appreciates in value. If the market goes down, your property depreciates with it. I think our entire being appreciates in value if we are appreciative. If we are ungrateful, we depreciate in value. I think our self worth and our net-worth have a lot to do with each other. If we are not grateful for our own existence, for the opportunity to receive money or provide a service, if we don't appreciate our clients or their needs, or if we don't appreciate money itself, it goes away. In order to build prosperity, you are wise to appreciate yourself and money. Having appreciation for yourself sometimes called self-worth, and having appreciation for your wealth sometimes called net worth are both powerful outcomes of the Gratitude Effect.

Money is always there, but the pockets change.
– GERTRUDE STEIN

I started unprofessional speaking when I was eighteen and then started professional speaking when I was twenty-three. I held my first paid seminars in the living room of my one bedroom apartment, and I used to place a little collection bowl out that said "Love Donations." I would speak to fifteen, twenty or thirty people, and only one or two people would leave any money in my "Love Donations" bowl. I would end up being paid five dollars for a two-hour seminar. This clearly wasn't working, so I changed the sign to "Minimum Love Donation – Five Dollars." Once again I got five or ten dollars for two hours of speaking. The following weekend I changed my little sign to read "Minimum Love Donation – Twenty Dollars," and I received twenty bucks. I finally got mad enough, so I put out a sign reading "Minimum Fee – Twenty Dollars." Guess what? Almost everyone attending put twenty bucks into the bowl, and I finally got it. I learnt my lesson. I realized that until I appreciate and value myself, I couldn't expect anybody else to do it. You have to appreciate yourself. If you don't feel worthy of receiving money, you won't receive it – pure and simple.

The universe is waiting for you to put a value on yourself, and you are magnificent. Try this affirmation and see if you feel different about who you are: "I am a magnificent being; I have a unique and exceptional service to offer, and I deserve to receive amazing compensation for my loving service."

Here is how to know if you financially value yourself. If you do, you pay yourself first, and if you don't, you pay yourself last. You automatically make payments according to the hierarchy of your values. For years I was paying everyone else ahead of me and could barely make ends meet, but then I became more financially savvy, and I have my lovely assistant to thank for it. She had only been working for me for a matter of weeks when one weekend she went to Las Vegas and got married in one of those quaint little chapels. The following Monday she came into the office and told me that she was quitting and wanted to get her remaining salary before the payday. Something clicked for me at that moment. I could see my investment of time and energy into my business and I could compare it to her investment. I thought that it wasn't fair that she be rewarded for her attitude before I got paid for my hard work. This is how I learnt to pay myself first, and to this day I am very thankful that she helped me learn this lesson.

I set up an automatic savings system that would withdraw money from my business account every month and would deposit it into my savings. It was pretty hard to start. I was very anxious, wondering if I could save two hundred dollars a month, but I decided to try. So, the moment I received the money, it would first go into my savings account, then I would pay my taxes, then my lifestyle, then my budgeted and prioritized business bills, and so on, according to what was most important for me. That was the beginning of my financial wealth.

All riches have their origin in mind. Wealth is in ideas – not money.

– ROBERT COLLIER

People who minimize themselves tend to want to give and become altruistic, thinking it is more of a blessing to give than to receive. They think other people are more important than them and deserve more than them, so they tend to work hard for other people. Those people who exaggerate themselves want to receive more than they want to give, so they tend to take have other people working intensely for them. Both types of people have a service they provide the world, and both experience pain and pleasure, and perceptions of success and failure. The question is – where do you want to play in this economic game? My observation is that the most fulfilling position is the centre point where you have fair exchange instead of trying to give or to get something for nothing. You provide a service, you get paid, and it's clean and clear.

We keep attracting people into our life who take our money until we become courageous enough and honest enough to stand up and say that we are valuable. We will keep attracting those takers until we own our self-worth. We would be wise to thank them because they are serving us by initiating an emotional reaction within us to the point where we say, "I'm worth more than that!" Appreciating yourself is the first part of the equation. The second part is understanding that money will go to you only if you appreciate it. If you don't, why would it come into your life?

Imagine this. You are in an art gallery, and you see an artist is standing next to his artwork. You walk up to his/her painting, shrug nonchalantly and walk away. Do you think this artist will be as inspired to create his next piece if people like you kept coming by? Probably not! But what would happen if you saw that person's art and said "Wow", gathered all your friends and all of you told the artist that you appreciated his painting? That could inspire that artist to create another masterpiece. The same is true in life. If someone has given us a gift, and we are appreciative of the gift, what happens? We are more likely to receive more gifts. Similarly, wealth goes where it is appreciated most.

A while ago my wife and I were at a friend's house in New York. We were sitting and chatting with him and his wife when he had an important phone call form Germany. He excused himself and went to another room to take the call. His wife was visiting with my wife, so I took a chance to explore his library. It was enormous. I noticed that one wall about ten feet high and about twenty feet wide was all filled with shelves of gold-embossed burgundy folders. I realized this was a catalogue of all his assets. I pulled out a folder to look at. This one was for a chandelier: two hundred seventy-five thousand dollars, the receipt, the insurance policy for it, and other documents. Next, the Egyptian hearth over the fireplace: three hundred eighty thousand dollars, its description, where he got it, the receipt, the insurance policy for it, etc. The paperwork for every single asset he had was organized and catalogued properly with utmost attention to detail. He also had copies of these records on his computer and in his safe. If something got broken or stolen, he would know exactly what to do and where to look for the documentation. It was all in order. Where there's order, there's clarity, and that's where the money flows.

Why You Shouldn't Become a Millionaire

I don't know much about being a millionaire,
but I'll bet I'd be darling at it.
– *DOROTHY PARKER*

I don't want any young person to strive to be a millionaire ever again. Maybe twenty years ago it might have been sufficient, but not today. A million is simply not enough financial wealth any more. Let me explain.

If you are going to live to be a hundred years old, wouldn't it be wise to plan your finances with this age number in mind, just in case you live that long? According to the consumer price index, in the last hundred years the average rate of inflation has been five per cent a year. It means that every fourteen to fifteen years the cost of living doubles. Let's imagine that you are twenty-five, and your real income today is x amount of dollars, let's say fifty thousand just to make it simple. I'm guessing that you want to have the same or better lifestyle when you retire, but in fourteen to fifteen years, it is going to take at least one hundred thousand dollars a year to maintain your current lifestyle. Some financial planners recommend that you plan to have your future passive investment income to be equal to what your actively earned income was. Fifteen more years brings us to two hundred thousand, and that's only thirty years from now. In another fifteen years, you will have to generate four hundred thousand, and in sixty years you will need eight hundred thousand dollars in order to maintain the lifestyle you enjoy today. So, if you are twenty-five and you want to live to be hundred, that's what it's going to take. It is hard to imagine, but it is true.

Let us crunch some more numbers. If by the time you retire, you want to save eight hundred thousand at six per cent rate, you have to have close to fourteen million in savings by then, and if you are not on track with saving this amount, you are potentially living in a fantasy. In other words, you think it's somehow going to happen without you having a savings schedule or an action plan to get there. I bet this doesn't make you feel great, but once you have this realization, you might put saving money higher on your priority list. What may also help you put money higher on your values list is writing down a couple hundred or even thousand reasons why saving money and building wealth will be of service to you, your loved ones, your community, and the world. It may take you three months, but it's worth it as it is going to change your life forever. That is why I want you to become at least a deca-millionaire. Why not? It's all intention. It doesn't take any more energy to create ten million dollars than it takes to create one. It's all in your mind. The Gratitude Effect, once initiated, demonstrates itself by inspiring financial plan of action.

Things don't change. We change.
– *HENRY DAVID THOREAU*

If you are not building enough wealth or not saving money, it simply means that you don't have a big enough reason. You don't believe me? Imagine you have children whom you love and who are your highest priority. If someone took them away from you and said, "Look, I'm taking your kids and I am going to hide them; you have thirty days to come up with a hundred thousand dollars or I will kill them." Imagine you don't have any savings, and you cannot borrow the money. You have to earn a hundred thousand dollars more, and you've got thirty days to do it. Would you come up with the money? Would you figure out a way? Of course you would, and I would, too, because all of a sudden you have a big enough reason for doing that. So, I want to leave you with the question: "Is there a shortage of money-making opportunities, or is there lack of will, vision, and appreciation for making money?" When you apply the Gratitude Effect to wealth building, your money begins to grow. In fact, your financial wealth won't increase unless you appreciate money. Listen to this story.

To Save, or Not to Save: That is the Question

Money talks... but all mine ever says is good-bye.
– *ANONYMOUS*

I had a chance to counsel with a doctor in the Mid-West. He had been in practice for eight years, and, at the end of those eight years, he was still in debt. He couldn't seem to find his way out of debt. His wife was aggravated and fed up with this situation. They both came in for a consultation.

I asked him, "Where does money fit in your value system?"

He said, "What does that mean?"

I said, "What's most important to you? Let us look at how you spend you time and your energy. Let us look at what your life demonstrates about your values."

"Well, one of the things I love is reading and studying spiritual texts. I love to learn about metaphysics and healing. I love socializing with my friends and talking to them about metaphysical ideas."

"Great, now we have found your focus. When you get the money, what do you do with it?"

"I buy books."

"What else do you do with it?"

"I go to seminars on healing."

"Do you have a savings programme?"

"No."

"This means that you value learning more than you value saving, and you value reading more than you value keeping money. Would you agree?"

"I guess I do."

"You see, if you don't value money highly enough to save it, it is probably not going to stay with you. It is going to pass right through your hands and into a new book, a new seminar, or into the hands of a new teacher who values it. You are going to distribute money according to the hierarchy of your values. Tell me honestly, what do you think about money?"

All of a sudden, he came up with all these beliefs about money he learnt as a child, "Money is not important, it's pure capitalism, it's not good, it's not spiritual, and I don't want it."

Aha! He had all these programmes running in his head.

I had to help him see it differently and to help him see the benefits of money. It took a while.

I asked him, "How much spiritual service could you provide to the world if you had a ton of money right now?"

"Probably more."

I asked, "So, are you holding back your spiritual service by not receiving money?"

"Maybe... yeah."

"Are you holding back your healing service because you don't know how to manage your money?"

"Yes."

"Is it keeping your clinic from being on the cutting edge?"

"I see."

I stacked up the downsides of not having appreciation for money, and he shifted his values that day. He broke through his guilt and started appreciating money. He then was on his way to activate the Gratitude Effect in relation to money.

Don't believe everything you think.
– *JENNY BOGART*

The counselling session took place on the weekend, and I asked him to go to the bank the following Monday to open a savings account and start saving. He looked at his wife to see what she thinks, and she said, "I've been trying to tell you this for years." She had been ready to build wealth for a long time, but she felt she could not do it alone.

He started saving, and at first he was ready to save only eighty dollars a month. You'd think a doctor can do better than that, but twenty dollars a week is a good start. It is wise to build your wealth progressively by adding no less than one per cent and preferably ten per cent to the amount you save every quarter. I talked to him half a year later, and he was already saving three hundred dollars a month. I'm going to meet him again next year, and if he stayed with the progressive plan I designed for him, he will be saving close to a thousand dollars a month at least. I know that if he stays with it, he is going to build real and lasting financial wealth.

This doctor couldn't start saving until he had a true appreciation for money, and a greater appreciation for what it represented. He didn't have gratitude for himself either. He was beating himself up. He couldn't move forward with his life because his finances were holding him back. Those who save money have money work for them. They become money's master. Those who don't have gratitude for money and don't save it, work their whole life for it and become its slave. It is that simple. It is up to you to decide whether you want to be a financial master or a financial slave. The only difference is in the level of appreciation for money and yourself.

A Little Too Late is Much Too Late

Minds are like parachutes; they work best when open.
– LORD THOMAS DEWAR

The sooner you start saving and investing your money, the greater the probability of growing a magnificent net worth. Why wait? There is no risk in doing it. The most challenging thing that could possibly happen is you might feel (in a moment of emotional uncertainty) that you have to take out the money you saved and invested to pay some of your bills. But when you appreciate and manage your money wisely, and focus on providing service, you receive more money to manage. When you have ten dollars in savings, you hang out with "tenairs"; when you have a hundred dollars saved, you hang out with "hundredaires"; a thousand dollars in savings and investments puts you in touch with "thousandaires"; a million – with millionaires, and a billion will naturally bring you into the circle of billionaires. When you are rubbing shoulders with "tenairs", you get ten-dollar ideas, ten-dollar opportunities and ten-dollar associations, but when you hang out with billionaires, you get billion dollar ideas, opportunities and associations.

People have all kinds of misconceived fears attached to the concept of saving and investing money. One misconception is the idea that saving money will block some form of universal flow of cash from moving and will make you stingy and stagnant. Possibly, if you hid your coins and cash in a pillow or a buried box, this concept might have some meaning.

It is wise to invest your money into real estate ventures, growing businesses, into creating new jobs and opportunities, and new services and products. So, you keep the money gratefully in motion. There is no hoarding any more. If we put it in a bank, it starts circulating again; if we invest it, it's in motion again – it's alive. The word "currency" comes from the word "current". I think of it as a current of spirit flowing through life. Just like electricity, money has a current. Electricity brings energy to things and gives us light, while the currency of money brings us life.

Would you Like to Jump from Fifty Thousand to a Million, or Would you Rather Continue Feeling Trapped?

Prosperity is a way of living and thinking, and not just money or things. Poverty is a way of living and thinking, and not just a lack of money or things.

– ERIC BUTTERWORTH

People sometimes break this current of spirit and feel stuck or trapped in life when they run out of strategies to get what they would truly love, when they feel that they have subordinated themselves to an outside authority, when they attempt to be someone they are not, and when they feel that they are emotionally disempowered. They are stuck only because they lose track of power and options they have. They really have much more power and more options than they know, but they have not used them because they don't see them. Ingratitude clouds their minds. The Gratitude Effect brings clarity of vision and opens new possibilities and helps people empower their lives.

Recently, while presenting one of my seminars called the Breakthrough Experience®, one gentleman said to me, "I just don't know how to make more than fifty thousand dollars a year."

I asked him if he felt that making money was truly high on his list of values. He said that it must not truly be. I asked him what strategies he intended to use to remedy his concern? He said he did not know what to do. I asked him if he knew anyone who was making much more than this amount. I asked him if he had ever asked them questions about how they did it, and what strategies they had used to make their money?"

"No, I just felt embarrassed."

I took him by his hand and said, "Let's go and talk to someone."

I put him in the centre of the room and had everyone give him ideas on how to make more money and share their stories on how they went from fifty thousand to two hundred or to five hundred thousand, whatever it was they were making. He got so many ideas that he was moved to tears by seeing all the new possibilities. He saw that he had had all these opportunities around him to learn, but he blocked them because he was afraid to be humble and ask for help. That's why the so-called low self-esteem part of us is helpful. It allows us to ask for help and often get it. If we think we are always right and we already know all the answers, sometimes we don't grow.

There is no reason you have to stop earning at fifty thousand dollars either. You probably want to set higher goals. Why not go for a million or two, or five or even much, much more?

How to be Grateful for Your Debt

Of all the attitudes we can acquire, surely the attitude of gratitude is the most important and by far the most life-changing.
– *ZIG ZIGLAR*

Now that we've talked about appreciating, making, saving and investing money, let's talk about a trickier subject – debt. There is a special way of dealing with debt, so it magically disappears from your head. You can reframe it in your mind so that if you owe money to a person or to a bank, think of them as your investors and be grateful for their belief in you. It's your chance to be grateful for that. Maybe they believed in you more than you did. Doesn't that deserve your gratitude?

Prosperity has a lot to do with gratitude. Many years ago, I read a book, *The Dynamic Laws of Prosperity* by Catherine Ponder, from whom I learnt to be grateful every time I wrote a check. I started doing that. I realized that if I was writing a check, in all likelihood I had already received a product or a service. I learnt it from my own experience that if I am grateful for the opportunity to write a check, it is easier to write it. It's a nice habit to include a little thank you note at the bottom of the check. People getting the check will likely be surprised by it, and it will probably make their day. They may even do this for someone else. Gratitude can certainly start a chain reaction. I call it the Gratitude Effect.

Studies have shown that if, after divorce, spouses are bitter and angry with each other, the probability of regular child support payments goes down. If the spouses part without bitterness and are grateful for each other, child support checks keep on coming. If you are grateful for the opportunity to pay the taxes, they are easier to pay. If you are grateful for the service someone provided to you or a loan someone gave you, it is easier to make the money to pay that person back. If you are grateful for your investment, it is easier to make profit from it. The Gratitude Effect changes the energy and allows you to make more money to pay back whatever you need to pay.

Gratitude Magic in Action

With more gratitude for money you materialize more money.
– *DR JOHN DEMARTINI*

Speaking about energy, I can't help sharing this story with you. One morning I woke up ungrateful. Even more than that – I was extremely irritated. When I came to my office, I was already aggravated with my staff, my patients, my family, a bunch of little things, and basically, everyone and everything around me. That morning I had what I call a "digito-cranial-rectalitis." It simply means that my thumb was in my mouth, and my head was up my... well, you can figure it out from the name. In other words, I was definitely ungrateful. As I walked into the office, I had a cloud around me, and one-by-one patients cancelled. It was almost like the universe made sure my patients didn't come in, so I didn't add to their disorder. I definitely did not have any healing energy that day. I was not in a gratitude attitude. I was in a pity-party, trauma-drama, ho-hum-dull-drum and stinking-thinking attitude.

There was a part of me that was so focused on feeling sorry for myself that I was almost glad the patients cancelled. I went into my private office and felt like I just wanted to curl up in a little ball on my desk with my arms around my knees. I was really down. I wanted everyone and everything out of my thoughts. I just wanted a quiet moment to myself. The whole office stopped.

I felt down and angry at the world. I felt that my staff members weren't doing their jobs; I was angry with the patients for canceling their appointments; I was angry with my wife because she did not want to understand my illusion. I was aggravated by the kids because they were noisy that morning. And then my inner voice spoke to me. It said, "Until you are grateful for what you have got, don't expect to receive more." It must have been a little whisper from my mom!

You can't 'take' a breath, your breath is given to you.
– SHIVA REA

Ingratitude is heavy; it weighs you down like gravity, but gratitude is light, and it radiates from you and expands your whole being. What I did after I heard this little voice was a great blessing. I went out through my little private door, walked down the sidewalk, and went to a little florist shop. I bought a bunch of flowers for everyone in my office, for some of the patients who were coming in later that day, and for my family. I probably got four-dozen roses. I came back, this time walking in through the business office and just started handing out a bunch of flowers to all my employees. I also gave a bunch of flowers to my assistant Kelly to put in a vase so I could take them home later that night. I gave everyone a flower and said, "I was having an ingratitude attitude, I was unrealistic and angry, consumed by my own drama, and the patients were running away from me because I was not in a healing energy state, but now I am ready. Thank you for being patient with me today. I know I wasn't easy to be around earlier." I went around and thanked my staff one by one, and gave each one of them a big hug. They were very surprised to say the least, and they told me, "It's OK. We all have days like this." I was grateful for them, they were grateful for me, and the energy has freed up. The telephone lit up. There was a radiation of love and gratitude in the room. It was palpable. We had people who cancelled in the morning come in the afternoon, and by then we had one of our bigger days. People who weren't even scheduled showed up.

Without question, the Gratitude Effect changed the energy. My ingratitude shut everything down, but my gratitude opened everything back up. I learnt that day that little gratitude goes a long way. I spent, maybe, a little over a hundred dollars on flowers, but got thousands in business. The Gratitude Effect pays.

Appreciate it Forward

All we see of someone at any moment is a snapshot of their life, there in riches or poverty, in joy or despair. Snapshots don't show the million decisions that led to that moment.

– *RICHARD BACH*

I know quite an interesting gentleman in New York City. My wife and I used to go out for dinner with him and his wife. We would go to Bice on 53rd Street, between Madison and Fifth Avenue. As we walked in the restaurant, he'd give a very nice tip to the person at the front door, then he would give a big tip to the waiter before we even started ordering and would say, "Thank you for the amazing service you are about to provide." He paid in advance, said "thank you" in advance. What kind of service do you think he received? The waiter and staff did amazing things for us. They did everything for this gentleman. The tip wasn't way excessive, it's just that he paid it in advance and thanked them in advance. Now they really wanted to take care of him. The Gratitude Effect was visible in the room because people could see how much attention he was getting, and because of this attention, everyone saw him as an important person.

I call it appreciating it forward, and I think it is a brilliant strategy. Last year, my business paid some of the bills in advance. We paid 2007 bills in 2006, and by doing so we received some extra special services. If you are grateful in advance for the service, you receive greater service. So go ahead and appreciate it forward. The ultimate destination of the gratitude journey is fulfillment and growth in all areas of life.

It is good to have an end to journey toward,
but it is the journey that matters in the end.
– URSULA K. LEGUIN

If you do not appreciate the idea of saving, spending wisely and managing money, if you do not appreciate what it can do for you and how it can serve other people, do not expect to have much wealth in your life. One of the most important things you can do, if you expect to have any wealth at all, is to learn to appreciate what it can offer. Wealth, in combination with a powerful vision and a cause can create masterpieces of service to the world. It can be used for positive or negative purposes based on various people's values. Wealth itself is neutral until someone judges the use of it. We must have appreciation for it before it comes into our hands. Make sure that you apply the Gratitude Effect to building your wealth and watching it grow.

Questions to Help you Stay Focused on Your Path to Prosperity

- What form of wealth do I already have that I can be grateful for?
- What form of wealth would I like to manifest?
- What have I done that allows me to feel worthy of having even greater wealth?

- What service can I provide to feel greater worth?
- What service can I provide that everyone in the world can benefit from?
- How can I translate this service into great fortune?
- What service can I provide that will bring wealth to others?
- How will saving money help me in my life?

Affirmations to Guide you on Your Journey

- I am grateful for the financial abundance that surrounds me and is available to me.
- Thank you for the abundance I have today.
- Thank you for the forms of abundance that are there, and thank you for those forms that are about to emerge.
- I am grateful for the opportunity to serve. The more I serve, the more I receive.
- I am grateful for my service that can bring me billions.
- I appreciate money for the service it provides.
- I appreciate money and how it raises my standard of living.
- I appreciate money because it provides opportunities for people.
- I love going to work. I love providing a service. And I love receiving economic rewards for it.

Action Steps to Speed up the Additional Wealth That's on its Way

Action Step 1. Today or tomorrow morning, open a personal, immortal savings/investment account. Have it automatically withdraw a fixed amount of money from your business account and put it into savings every month. Choose the amount based on how much you appreciate your business, yourself, your clients, or your service. The more you appreciate those, the higher amount you will set. See how much you can save based on how much gratitude you feel. See if you can increase your gratitude and your savings every quarter. Once you accumulate some wealth, you will see that wherever money accumulates, that's where money goes. Every time you write a thank you note, put a dollar into your savings account. It's an inspirational investment. If you can write twenty notes at night, put twenty dollars into you account. Ten notes – ten dollars. See if you can draw in more wealth this way with the Gratitude Effect.

Action Step 2. In your head, go through your life and write down every single thing that you have ever done and considered a mistake or a "screw-up" and have never felt grateful for. Go through this list, and, for each action that you can't appreciate, write down twenty-five ways of how it served you and twenty-five ways of how it served others. It doesn't have to be limited to twenty-five. You can write hundreds. This may take some time, but it's worth it. It will help you clear out all the shame and all the guilt associated with what you thought were mistakes, but in fact were just your unbalanced perceptions. This exercise will help you appreciate yourself just the way you are, minus the baggage of your self-deprecating perceptions. When you do, you will be even more willing to receive money. This exercise will help you increase your feeling of worthiness.

Action Step 3. Think about your debt and in your mind thank your investors for believing in you. Then break your debt down to how much you want to pay back in a month, a week, a day, an hour, then convert these to units of service and focus on service to people. If you focus on service, your debt goes away. If you focus on debt, your service goes away.

Action Step 4. Money automatically flows to where it is appreciated most and to whoever appreciates it most. This exercise is aimed at helping you increase its flow into your life. Write down how saving money and building wealth can be of service to you, your loved ones, and the world. Write down what you can do with the money that you can be grateful for. How will it serve you, your loved ones, and the world? Write down how it is of value, so you can appreciate money.

Don't stop at three items. Write one hundred reasons and one hundred benefits of how wealth coming into your hands could benefit you and the world you love. The more connections you see between money and honouring your values, the faster it will come to you. Appreciate life! Appreciate wealth! And watch how with the Gratitude Effect it will appreciate in your hands!

CHAPTER 6

There's No Place Like Home

How to Promote Someone from a Pain in the Neck to the Person of Your Dreams

If you judge people, you have no time to love them.
– *MOTHER THERESA*

Have you ever tried telling someone close to you to change? How did it work for you? All we need to do in order to change someone into the person of our dreams is to adjust our vision as soon as possible. I don't tire of saying that all human beings want to be loved and appreciated for who they are. They live according to their values, and in order to be grateful for them, it is wise to learn their values. If we want them to live according to our values, we will be unappreciative and, I guarantee, frustrated. When we understand why they act the way they do because we know their values, it is easier to figure out how this serves us. No matter what they do, it's wise to ask, "How does it serve me?" The more we ask this question, the more grateful for them we will become.

If you would love to have your relationship partner or spouse do something special, it is wise not to just project your expectations on to them without considering their values and needs. Communicate the action you would like to see in terms of your partner's values, explaining how it is going to serve him/her. Your partner or spouse will appreciate your effort, and you will be grateful for their response. The art of communicating in terms of each other's values is the secret. People are not appreciative when we project our unrealistic expectations onto them. When we do project such expectations onto others, we receive responses that can often leave us ungrateful or frustrated in turn. And if we end up ungrateful for them and for ourselves, we would probably end up projecting this dissatisfaction onto even more people.

If, on a daily basis, you kept an ongoing list of what you could be grateful for in each of your family members, you would give yourself a gift of a more empowered family communication. You would give yourself a gift of the Gratitude Effect. You would begin to see how they serve you just the way they are. This includes the challenges that come from them too. If your husband leaves his socks on the floor, ask how it serves you. If you see how it serves you instead of their actions running your life, you will set yourself free. Gratitude occurs when the mind is balanced. When we see more benefits than drawbacks, we feel infatuated. When we see more drawbacks than benefits, we feel resentful. When we are balanced, we feel gratitude and love.

You are Just Perfect for Me

Love all God's creation, the whole and every grain of sand of it. Love every leaf, every ray of God's light. Love the animals, love the plants, love everything. If you love everything, you will perceive the divine mystery in things. Once you perceive it, you will begin to comprehend it better every day. And you will come at last to love the whole world with an all-embracing love.

– *FYODOR DOSTOYEVSKY*

Often, the people who are closest to us are the hardest ones to love and appreciate. Let's talk about family. Everyone has a mother, a father, a brother, a sister, a son, a daughter, and grandparents at all times. And I mean always. Even if your parents or grandparents pass away, someone else will fill in that void. If your child goes off to college and disappears from your life, someone else will take on that role. Nothing is ever missing. It's just changing. We would be wise to be grateful for the many evolving forms of our family. In our immediate family dynamics as well as in our extended "cosmic family", there is always a full display and balance of opposites. When we see it, there is an awakening of true gratitude.

I am very grateful for my parents. My dad was a philosopher who never quite figured out how to make a full time living doing it, and so I ended up doing that. My mom was a Christian Science healer. She didn't know how to make a living doing that, but I did. I am grateful for their combination. They were the perfect parents to get me to where I am now. I got both support and challenge from them. If my dad hadn't challenged me when I was a young teenager, I wouldn't have left home and wouldn't have become as independent as I am today.

I was thirteen and about to leave the house, when my dad said, "You are not going out tonight. You are staying home." I have to let you in on a secret – my girlfriend was waiting for me in a nearby city, and I wanted to kiss her more than anything in the world, and to me this was the opportunity I didn't want to miss. So I said to my dad, "No, I'm going out." There was no way I was going to pass up this chance to be intimate. I didn't want to tell my dad about it, but I didn't want to stay home either. We had a little argument, and so he said, "If you leave now, don't come back." I don't think he meant it, but he just tried to test me like any dad would do. I said, "Okay," packed my bag and left. He didn't expect this. As for me, I just wanted to hug and kiss her.

That was the beginning of my independence. After this, my dad and I got along on an entirely new level. He realized that his son had grown up. From that day on, he treated me like a completely different person. But I had to challenge him first to get my independence.

He also had to challenge me, so I could grow. When I was in my twenties, I had to get a business loan for opening my practice. He co-signed for part of it but charged me four per cent on top of 7.5 per cent the bank was charging. So, my interest rate became 11.5 per cent. He just wanted to make sure I learnt the consequences of borrowing money. He challenged me, but he also supported me. He did both. He was a perfect father for me. His presence definitely assisted me in awakening to the Gratitude Effect.

More Perfect People Undercover

Every man has his follies – and often they are the most interesting thing he has got.

– JOSH BILLINGS

Recently I worked with a lady who had breast cancer. She thought that her father was a violent brutal bastard, mean as can be. But from my experience of working with thousands of people, I know for sure that one polarity cannot exist by itself. So, I asked her, "Who was very supportive and overprotective of you in your family?" She told me that her mother, her grandmother, and her aunt were always very sweet to her and were trying to meet her every need.

I asked, "Had you stayed with them in that environment, do you think you would have become very dependent? Can you see that your father, by being who he was, forced you to grow up and become your own independent person who could stand up for herself?"

"I guess, you are right."

"What do you do today?"

"I am a consultant to CEOs of major corporations."

"Do you think that your father might have trained you to not be intimidated, be firm, confront things head on, fight back, and stand your ground?"

"You are so right, I can see it now."

"Did you ever thank your father for getting a career you love and learning the leadership skills from him?"

"I never saw it this way before."

"How do you know that it is not a gift he gave you?"

"Well, I'm starting to think that maybe it is."

"When you were little, did you have a friend who, you thought, had a better deal in her family?"

"Yes, I had a girlfriend who had a father I wanted. He seemed to be very kind and supportive of her."

I said, "Would you trade places with her today?"

"No! In fact, she is almost forty and still living at home with her parents."

"If your father was sitting right next to you now, what would you tell him?"

"Well, I have other issues with him. Sometimes, he was mean and abusive to my mom."

"Was your mom a meek, passive, partially disempowered

person who was beating herself up and who wouldn't stand up for certain things she believed?"

"Yeah."

"And did his actions finally get her frustrated enough to finally stand up for herself and gain some strength and to mature?"

"That's exactly what she did. She finally got to a point where she was ready to break up with him and she got her strength back."

I asked, "And did he soften then?"

"Right from the time when he hit fifty, and my mom has become more aggressive since that time."

"Have you been surrounded by people who supported your fantasy?"

"Yes, my friends have all supported my idea that my dad was a monster."

"There is no parent who doesn't love his or her children. And there's no child who doesn't love his or her parents. That's the truth of their hearts. Your father played a role in your life, and because of him you are now independent, driven and high achiever."

She finally saw that her dad's aggression was a gift, and she couldn't hold her tears. That was a major breakthrough for her. The next day she called her father. Thus, both of their lives were impacted by the Gratitude Effect.

Life is under no obligation to give us what we expect.

– MARGARET MITCHELL

You always have a perfect balance in your family dynamic. And the wisdom is embracing everyone's role, the mean and the kind, support and challenge, all the opposites. One person may be working, another – doing the repairs on the house, yet another – cooking or mowing the lawn. All of them are balancing your family dynamics, and it's easy to become grateful for their role in your family if you just take the time to look.

For example, my parents didn't travel, but I'm travelling the world. So I am grateful for them being homebound because it allowed me to travel. I am grateful for some people in my family being the socialites, so that I can be the intellectual. You can play out the opposites in the family dynamics and think how you can be grateful for the opposites. Look for the expression/repression dynamics in the family. Whenever someone in the family is repressing something, someone else is expressing it. You can thank the other person for playing out the opposite role, so you can be who you are. Our family is constantly teaching us the many ways of living with the Gratitude Effect.

The Three People I am Most Grateful for

One hundred years from now, it will not matter what my bank account was, how big my house was, or what kind of car I drove. But the world may be a little better, because I was important in the life of a child.

– *FOREST WITCRAFT*

Interacting with our children brings about some of the most difficult lessons but may also create some of the most rewarding moments. I was very lucky because I really didn't have any big challenges with my kids. They haven't done anything I haven't done, so no matter what it was, I knew it was just a stage in their life. Another year or two, and they would be past it. After all, I was living on the streets by the time I was a teenager.

My beautiful daughter, Breccia Aurora Demartini, has been the leading socialite, party lover and determined and outgoing extravert of the family. She courageously lets people know what she thinks and how she feels. Her initials comically spell B.A.D. I didn't realize initially that we had named her with these initials, but she would bring it to my attention and would capitalize on that periodically. Early on I knew she would be like Albert Einstein, the great challenger. I also knew that would probably make her a great entrepreneur and leader. I knew she would stand up to authority and probably become one in turn. Indeed, when I played the role of the authority, she would stand up to me. Occasionally, this would be frustrating because she wouldn't always want to do what I would tell her to do, so I would sometimes become impatient. I was challenged by her when she was trying to do things her way. That used to push my buttons, but she didn't really do anything major. I was being trained to communicate more effectively in her values, and she made sure I experienced love on a much more profound level. I knew that she would probably go far. She is certainly driven. She is determined and will not let anything stop her. Her creative ways of getting what she wants are numerous and astounding. It is inspiring to watch her mature and bloom as a young woman.

My other beautiful daughter, Alana Joy Demartini, is writing, and studying photography, philosophy, marketing, journalism and business. I am also inspired by her. By the time she was eighteen, she knew enough about my teachings to be able to assist me with one of my seminars and with the facilitation of the Demartini Method®. It was in Toowoomba, Queensland, Australia. I had about forty-five people in the seminar, and I was running late into the evening. Alana started facilitating the attendees through the Method. She did an amazing job helping people open their hearts to the experience of gratitude and love in spite of their many challenges. She went around and started working with four of the attendees individually. She had been to some of my classes before and had observed me work, and learnt what to do. Although she was a teenager, she was helping people who were twice or three times her age to dissolve their dramas and tragedies and become grateful for their lives. She truly amazed me that day.

Having children makes you no more a parent than having a piano makes you a pianist.
– *MICHAEL LEVINE*

Parents live vicariously through their children. Everything parents repress, kids express. My handsome, long-haired, teenage son, Daniel David Demartini, is presently expressing some of my musical repressions, and in some respects he is hundred and eighty degrees opposite to me. He loves writing lyrics and creating rock music for his heavy metal band. Daniel's dream is to be a rock star. He takes many of the concepts, ideas and words I use in my teachings, reverses them or uses antonyms and puts them into his lyrics and sings about them. I think it's ingenious. I was just like him when I was his age. I am amazed by his vocabulary and degree of intensity and intelligence.

I am grateful for him because he is expressing some of the desires I have been repressing or disowning. He is living out some of my dreams that I had when I was a teenager but never got around to realizing them. I was in a little rock band but didn't go very far with it. Now he is carrying that part of my dream out. I am grateful that I can delegate to my kids aspiration I didn't get around to doing, including some of my teenage dreams.

I think it's inspiring to be able to openly express your love and gratitude for each other in the family. As I don't see them every day, they have become very close to me. However, there are also other times when they wish I were there to help, but I'm not. No matter what you do, they both like and dislike you and that is what makes up the two sides of love and helps awaken the Gratitude Effect.

Each morning I go down my gratitude list and become thankful for all my blessings, and the first place I start with is my children. I am grateful for them, and I dedicate my life to helping them find their mission and fulfill their dreams. I am very grateful for the opportunity to learn from them and to help them live their lives to the fullest.

On Parents, Bears and Teenage Hitchhikers

We are all born for love. It is the principle of existence, and its only end.
– *BENJAMIN DISRAELI*

Adults can be stuck with their fixed notions of what the world is like, but children can teach us a thing or two because they can capture the simple truths of life intuitively. I was working with a four-year old child whose father had just passed away. Everyone around him was concerned about his well-being because he became really introverted. He would hide in his room frequently and would hardly want to talk to anyone.

I asked him, "What do you think about your dad?"

"Well, he is gone."

"But where is he now? In what form? See, daddies don't leave. They just change form. Who has become more like your dad? Is there a new uncle in your life? Or has your brother become more like your dad? Is your mom acting more like your dad? Who?"

He said, "My bear."

"You've been talking to your bear?"

"Yeah."

"What kind of conversation did you have?"

"My bear tells me what I am to do. He says, 'It's time to go to bed; it's time to clean up,' and other things."

He said that his daddy got him the bear some time ago, but he hadn't played as much with it until his daddy passed away.

"So, your dad has changed into your bear, and now you can keep him in your arms at night?"

He nodded his head. He was in a different mood now. He

had already figured out the way to compensate for his loss, and his family was more concerned about him than he was. When we left his room, he went to his mom and told her, "Daddy has been talking to me through my bear."

She looked at me for an explanation. I told her that since his father had passed away, her son had been talking to his bear as if he was his daddy, and the bear had been talking back to him, giving him advice and answering his questions. The bear was doing everything his dad used to do. He told him to make sure he brushed his teeth, made his bed, etc.

I told her that I helped her son find all the missing parts of his daddy in her, her family, her friends, and his bear. I also told her that there would be the whole group of people representing a father figure in his life. He might have a male coach or a male teacher, or her new husband or his older friend who would represent his father because mothers and fathers never go away – they just change forms. This realization of transformation awakened in her son and in the entire family the Gratitude Effect.

One word frees us of all the weight and pain of life; that word is love.
– SOPHOCLES

After my parents dropped me off on the freeway, different surrogate mothers and fathers kept manifesting all throughout my journey. Whenever I hitchhiked, I frequently ran into parent figures picking me up. At times I would get picked up by a whole family that would help me for two or three days. Life would provide me with people nurturing and/or challenging me, buying food for me and caring for me, and I felt intuitively grateful for them as if they were acting out parts of my parents.

We never know how our sincere gratitude is going to affect others. The Gratitude Effect certainly goes a long way. I was about seventeen years old and had just learnt how to meditate from Paul Bragg. One day, during my meditation, I got a clear message, "It's time to go see your parents. You are to help them with their health." I always kept enough money in a small local bank in Hawaii to make sure I could fly to the mainland. Back then all you needed was eighty-six dollars.

I hitchhiked to Honolulu and flew back to California. When I got there, my old friend Jackie came to pick me up from the airport. We went to his house where I met his parents. I stayed with them for three days. As I was into natural foods, fasting and yoga at that time, I got them to eating natural and raw foods. At first they had a lot of gas problems and cramps from eating all those fresh raw salads I prepared for them, but they got over it, and it gave us something to laugh about. I would make a big salad, and we would sit and talk about surfing and health, and I would share everything I had learnt from Paul Bragg with Jackie and his parents. They were my family at that time.

When I was ready to hitchhike to Texas, Jackie's mother gave me a ride to the freeway. It was early spring, and there was a big northern storm moving South-East across California and the rest of the United States. She took me to the edge of the storm, right where it just started raining and just like my parents, who had dropped me off on the freeway several years ago, she dropped me off on the freeway on my journey back home.

The first ride I got was in a police car. I thought, "Oh, great. Now I have to hear about the laws of hitchhiking from the police. They are going to give me a hard time." But I was surprised as a father-like man gave me a ride farther out of the city so I wouldn't get drenched. They took me quite a number of miles ahead of the storm. And every time I could see the storm about to come, I would be offered another ride. I raced this Northern Cold Front storm across the States. Somehow I seemed to miraculously get a ride right before the storm would hit; I received all kinds of amazing rides, and that's when I realized that somehow the universe was taking care of me. I could feel it, and was inwardly grateful. This repeated synchronicity I felt was due to the Gratitude Effect.

Our first teacher is our own heart.
– AMERICAN INDIAN PROVERB

I got home safe and decided to write a thank you letter to Jackie's mom. I had good handwriting because I practised a lot in elementary school, but I didn't know a lot of grammar or too many words so my mom had to help me write it. I sent it off, and that was the end of it. Or so I thought.

Three years ago, I received my letter back. I was on my way from Texas to Australia and passed through California. Two days before my flight, my surfer friend Jackie called me and said, "John, I have something for you. When are you coming to California?" I said, "In two days." He said, "My mom has just passed away, and when she did, she had something in her hand that she wanted me to give you. He came to the LAX airport in Los Angeles and gave me the letter I wrote to his mom thirty-two years ago. She died holding my letter in her hands. This is how it goes:

I want to thank you for all that you did for me while I was there, especially being yourselves and allowing me to stay there. I hope my nutrition crisis didn't upset you and your family. I'm sort of pushy. Too pushy, really. But I never leave my diet, and it was proven most beneficial to me because of my strychnine poisoning. But anyway, I got home safe and sound and am enjoying it. I am planning on staying here for

quite a while. Well, there's not much I can say, but thank you for everything, and God is looking over us.
Take care.

Yours truly,
John

P.S. I appreciate the ride to the freeway. It really helped.

Why Can't You Just Stop Being Yourself?

> *You will find as you look back upon your life that the moments when you have truly lived are the moments when you have done things in the spirit of love.*
>
> *– HENRY DRUMMOND*

We had a discussion about children, talked about parents and parent figures – why leave out our significant others? I met a lady who was "committed" to her marriage. When she got married, she vowed, "That's it. I am going to die married. No matter what happens. That's the way the church teaches it. And if I don't stay married, I will go to hell." Her belief was that she was going to heaven if she kept her commitment, and if she didn't... well, we'll never know because the last time I checked, she was still keeping her word. Meanwhile, her husband has had multiple affairs; he doesn't work; he is an alcoholic, and she has endured the most amazing trials in her marriage. She is just going to stay in her marriage because she believes that the pain of going to hell is greater than the pain and suffering she is going through right now. She has cancer and other health issues, she has lived much of her entire life holding herself back, but she is committed to her belief system. It's her value system that she is committed to, not actually her marriage.

Commitment is actually not the most accurate word. Because you are ultimately only "committed" to your highest values – consciously or unconsciously – committing to anything else that is not truly aligned to your highest values will probably turn out to be futile or at least frustrating. The funny thing is, when it is aligned to what is truly most important, you don't need to consciously "commit". You are already living it. When someone says, "I'm going to marry you. I'm committed to you," it's not true. That person is not committing to you – he/she is committing to his/her highest values, and as long as you are supporting those values, he/she is probably going to be with you. If you were to challenge those values long enough, he/she just might go somewhere else.

People are only committed to their highest values, and if their relationship happens to be their highest value, they are committed to it, but only as long as it reflects their values. People will be true to their real values. That's why I don't expect people to commit to me. Instead, I expect them to live according to their values. This may be one of the more challenging aspects of the Gratitude Effect, but it's true nonetheless. If I love someone, I am prepared to love and appreciate their values too. As long as I help them live according to their highest values more than anyone else, they act as if they are "committed" to me.

We don't see things as they are. We see them as we are.
– ANAÏS NIN

A lovely lady named Tina asked me to consult with her son who was into computers and videogames. She was frustrated because he was old enough to be working, but he didn't have the slightest desire to do so – at least at a job she labeled work. To her, he was "just sitting all day in front of the computer being lazy." She said, "It drives me nuts."

It turned out that he was actually quite a genius when it came to computers. From a conversation with him, I learnt that he taught himself software development and opened an online software and website development company. She had no idea. She was way behind the times probably because of her repression and fear associated with new computer technology. He was excelling at computers. He is very accomplished today. As he began to make money with his business, Tina realized that his "sitting at home all day in front of the computer and being lazy" was the training he was getting for subsequent achievements, but at the moment she wasn't aware of it.

Sometimes, in family dynamics, we don't see the benefits of someone's actions. We don't see how it is serving us. We would be smart to realize that people are going to live according to their values, and not according to ours. When we project our values on them, we don't appreciate them for who they are, and we miss a chance to be grateful. The Gratitude Effect is awakened when we come to appreciate the magnificence and uniqueness of other's values.

We often forget that everyone has different values and that people don't see the world the same way we do. We keep projecting our understanding onto them, and when they don't match up, we get angry with them. That's a form of ignorance because we ignore their values. Is it a surprise, then, that we run into emotional reactions? Any time we expect people to abandon their values and adopt ours, we are setting ourselves up to feel betrayed.

We have been trained to believe that we are right, but we have not necessarily been trained to be grateful and loving. The less training we've had in love, the more we will try to be right. Just like in sales – if we don't know how to sell, we are going to keep projecting what we think people need. Instead of finding out what they feel they need. It takes some training. It all goes back to the old golden rule: Treat others the way you want to be treated. We want someone to ask us what we need before they try to sell us something. If we do the same, we will go and grow farther.

Ever After and Beyond

True love never lives happily ever after – true love has no ending.
– K. KNIGHT

My wife passed away nearly three years ago. We both discovered quite late that she had advanced cancer, and then for privacy purposes she chose to keep it a secret because she didn't want attention from the media. Shortly before she died, we had a very special conversation. We sat at home and had a beautiful evening of reminiscing about all the great moments we shared and all the things we had the opportunity to do during our life together. We were both filled with gratitude for each other. We scanned through these truly amazing twelve and a half years. We had traveled the world, lived on a luxury ship and in beautiful penthouses all over the world, met amazing people, many of them celebrities, and visited royalty. We both had written books, were blessed by the opportunity to do what we loved doing, did interviews together, spoke together, served many causes… We had experienced so much together. So, that night we just sat there remembering our life together and letting hours pass by. Her name was Athena Starwoman, and that night she said to me, "I am so grateful that I was able to meet my Starman before I died."

Later that night I had another speaking engagement to fly to, so I had to leave shortly after our conversation. When I went to bed that night, I was at a different location, away from her. About two hours after falling asleep, I was "awakened" by her. All of a sudden, I saw a clear image of her in my mind and heard her say very clearly, "Make sure when I pass, to thank these four people," and she told me in detail what to say to four people because she couldn't reach them. You will be as surprised as I was to learn that the day she passed, it was those four people who called, and I got to say a special "thank you" to each one of them.

When we are in a state of gratitude, we access a higher communication system. This was an example the telepathic, non-local, quantum Gratitude Effect. She was a very intuitive person, and on the day she passed, those four people just "happened" to call not even knowing she was sick.

People ask me, "How can you be grateful when your wife passed?" I was very grateful. I was grateful for the years we had together. I was grateful that her passing was smooth and fast, and that she did not have to go through some of the major challenges that others with her condition more commonly go through. Her death was very gracious. She wanted to leave beautiful, and she left beautiful. Gratitude still connects me to her through love.

Sometimes the heart sees what is invisible to the eye.
– H. JACKSON BROWN, JR

Athena and I had talked about death before she passed and transformed. We both agreed that whoever was going to pass first wanted the other person to go on with his/her life and live to the fullest. Six weeks before her passing, we held hands, and looked into each other's eyes and she said, "It's now come a time when you're going to have to find you a nice, new, young Stargirl." At that moment, it was the last thing on my mind, but three weeks after she had passed, something happened that is worth telling.

I was speaking at a large conference in Las Vegas, and at the end of it, I was signing books for about three hours. At some point, the next person in line was this lovely lady. She had a big hat on, was all fashion savvy and looked like a model. She came up to me, and I asked her, "And your name, please," and she said, "Starr."

I looked up and instantly remembered what my wife had

said just nine weeks earlier. It took me a second to process it, and then I asked her, "Do you mind sticking around for a few minutes, I would love to talk to you about your name." I learnt that Starr was her real name. We spent the afternoon together talking, and then I didn't see her for two months. After two months, I saw her for lunch, and another month later I saw her for another lunch. Then I asked her if she would like to go to on a trip to Australia with me, and it's been nearly three years since we've been together.

The moment you have in your heart this extraordinary thing called love and feel the depth, the delight, the ecstasy of it, you will discover that for you the world is transformed.

– J. KRISHNAMURTI

There is another twist to this story. When Starr and I travelled to Australia, we visited the penthouse that my wife Athena and I had. I hadn't been back since her passing, so the penthouse was exactly the way that we had left it. Shortly after we arrived, I went into the bathroom to put my toiletries up, and she went to put her things into the bedroom closet. Then I saw her quickly back out of the closet and sit on the edge of the bed with a strange look on her face. She looked a bit shocked and puzzled.

I asked, "Are you OK? What is it?"

She said, "I just need to sit here for a second."

"What happened?"

She said, "Well, I went into the closet, and I saw your wife's clothes, and thirteen of her outfits are identical to mine. Same brand, same colour, same size, same everything. Fifteen pairs of shoes in there are identical to mine. I have exactly the same outfits and shoes, and it just shook me."

I suddenly got chills up my spine. Then we went into the

bathroom, and she had some of exactly the same make-up, hair accessories, and other toiletries. We went downstairs, and she had exactly the same china and crystal as we did. We had a white and gold Rolls Royce that we drove, and she drove a white and gold Jaguar Classic. Athena and I lived on a condominium ship called The World that circumnavigates the world, and she used to live on the QM ship with her former boyfriend. Apparently those two ships travel to the same ports, so my late wife and Starr ended up going to the same boutiques and choosing some of the same outfits and accessories. There we were, trying to take in this amazing synchronicity.

I am open to the guidance of synchronicity,
and do not let expectations hinder my path.
– DALAI LAMA

There is never a loss, but a transformation, and when you love someone, that person is never lost, just transformed, and you can feel his/her presence. I am grateful for over twelve and a half years I spent with Athena, and I am also grateful for Starr, who has been in my life since that time. I went from Starwoman to Stargirl. She also writes books like my wife used to; she is into fashion and does modeling just like my wife used to, and the synchronicities don't stop there. I think that because I was grateful and felt this non-local love, the universe has transformed this love energy and manifested it into another new vital form. The Gratitude Effect opens your heart to new possibilities that you don't get to experience otherwise. The next step in my life always unfolds when I am grateful for what I have. Then I get something even more magnificent to be grateful for.

Gratitude allows you to enter into a state that the philosopher and theologian Thomas Aquinas called synchronicity, and to see the opportunities that you would normally miss otherwise. When you are ungrateful, you don't see them, so you can't act upon them.

Today, Starr has pictures of my late wife, Athena, and I together in her apartment in Houston, Texas. When people come in to see the apartment and they see my former wife's pictures, they are surprised and ask why the pictures are there. Starr just says, "Because we are all connected. He loves me now, but this is someone he loved before, and it's important to me."

When I first met my late wife Athena, I had a similar synchronicity. I found out that she had been married to a man named Bob, who had surfed with one of my surfing buddies in Hawaii. In fact, he was the best friend of my surfing buddy. Even though she lived in Australia, we had mutual friends in Hawaii. Apparently we were connected for twenty years through these people without knowing each other.

With gratitude, the entire world suddenly becomes your friend and family.
– *DR. JOHN DEMARTINI*

Family means different things to different people. Some people have immediate families that include a spouse, their children, and parents, while others are involved in family structures of a more unusual kind. Some people regard those who reside in their city, country or even across the world as their extended family. Your personal sense of family may take any form suitable to your taste. And even if you consider yourself a loner, you still have intimate or more distant family-like connections to others. You are never on your own – after all, we are all part of the cosmic family. You are partly who you are as a result of your participation in a greater global family dynamic. And everyone in your family, both the immediate real and the extended global one, whoever and however they are, helps make your overall character possible. That is worth being grateful for. And, of course, thank yourself for the magnificent role you play in your own magnificent makeup!

Questions to Help You See Your Family Differently

- What am I most grateful for in relationship to my mother?
- What am I most grateful for in relationship to my father?
- What am I most grateful for in relationship to each of my siblings?
- What am I most grateful for in relationship to my grandmother?
- What am I most grateful for in relationship to my grandfather?
- What am I most grateful for in relationship to my spouse/partner?
- What am I most grateful for in relationship to my children?

Affirmations to Open Your Heart to Gratitude

- My gratitude is the key that opens the gateway to my loving heart.
- I love myself exactly as I am. I am perfect the way I am.
- No matter what I have done or not done I am worthy of love.
- I love my family members; for, they are my perfect balance.
- My love for others and for myself is the answer of answers to all my questions of questions.
- Just as I demonstrate my love through my unique values, so do others.
- The more love I give, the more love I receive.
- I love unconditionally with my heart.

- No matter what happens I know it is a lesson in love.
- Within me and around me there is nothing but love.
- My love reigns supreme over all of my emotions.
- I focus on love; for, I know that anything unloved runs my life.
- I give others and myself enough space and time for love.
- My love brings whomever I love into my presence.
- I take time for the ones I love.
- I honour both sides of the ones I love.
- I love catching the ones I love at their best.
- If I were available I would ask myself out.
- I love my family members just the way they are.
- I listen to my heart and experience the most beautiful and intimate relationships.
- My heart guides me to say exactly what is wise and loving.

Exercises to Help You Appreciate Yourself and Others

Exercise 1. Thank You Letter

Write a thank you letter to everyone in your life to whom you haven't said thank you. A telephone or an email will work too.

Exercise 2. Brief Version of the Demartini Method®

- What specific trait pushes your buttons when you see it in other people?
- Who sees this trait in you? Write down names of at least twenty people. Don't think or say that you don't have this trait. That would be denial. Everyone has every trait, just in his or her own unique form. Keep looking until you see it.
- When did you display it? Think of at least twenty occasions.
- At whom was it directed?

- How does this trait in you serve others?
- How does this trait in others serve you?

Exercise 3. This one is a lot of fun to do at your family dinner table. Ask everyone to write seven things they are grateful for in everyone else at the table and then ask them to speak the words of gratitude about one another. Ask your kids, "What are you grateful for in your brother or sister today?" It's not always easy, and I guarantee that someone will say, "I can't think of any." You just have to keep asking them to look. If you can't come up with seven, do five or do three. Do something, and you will feel the magic of it right there at that family dinner as it opens up the doorway for more heartfulness and more communication.

CHAPTER 7

If All Pulled in One Direction, the World Would Keel Over

The World is a Jigsaw Puzzle, or Don't Underestimate the Value of Your So-called Enemies

It is the enemy who can truly teach us to practise the virtues of compassion and tolerance.
– DALAI LAMA

The world is made of a full bouquet of complementary opposites. For every pro-this, there is a pro-that. For every anti-this, there's an anti-that. The world is inherently balanced, and whenever we run into our assumed opposite, that person is simply teaching us that we have possibly become a bit rigid in our thinking, or we have boxed ourselves into a limited belief system. If our global leaders become too rigid or fundamental in their ideologies and thinking, they predictably attract their balancing opponents. If one thinks that he/she will win the battle and rid the other of his/her foolish thinking, the other will emerge in opposition and compensation. The truth is that we can never truly conquer the opposition because what we condemn we breed. All we attract by being stubborn and rigid is a humbling experience. That is the magnificence of the balance of life.

We are going to attract our assumed opposites until we realize that they are just human beings with their own values who are serving the world as much as we are. They both support and challenge, and build and destroy. All opposites are necessary in the world, and our so-called opponents are just as valuable as we are. Society is built like a jigsaw puzzle where every piece is unique and invaluable. If every piece were exactly the same, I would take it back to the store and demand a refund. We need our opposites in order for the whole puzzle to fit together and for the big picture to emerge. The Gratitude Effect emerges when we embrace both sides wholeheartedly.

Leadership opportunities have a lot to do with our values. If we believe that only certain types of people are good, we will be limited by their number in the world to potentially follow our leadership. If we believe that only people from certain locations are good, then we will be limited by the number of people only in those locations. If we see that everyone in the world has both sides and is not better or worse than others, we have discovered a greater possibility for us to lead. Remember, a principle I had shared earlier, "Anything you have an emotion about runs you. Anything that you love, you get to run." In this case we automatically grow in our leadership capacity to the degree we can appreciate and love people – from both sides of any issue.

We cannot manage people in a company or a political party if we cannot appreciate their different roles and values. Every job needs a certain value system to carry it out. A person who wants to work in a factory has a different set of values than the person who wants to work at the top of a corporation. All the values are needed to fill in all the different gaps throughout all the different levels of corporations or society. We want to be grateful for all the pieces of the puzzle. The business world and society couldn't function if everyone had the exact same values.

The only abnormality is the incapacity to love.
– *ANAÏS NIN*

It would be like one of the Twilight Zone episodes where this guy gets up in the morning, and all day people around him become exactly like him. When he comes out of his apartment, it's the person next to him in the elevator and the concierge in his apartment building whom he doesn't like. He says, "I wish everyone was more like me." Then he comes out to the street and bumps into someone and says, "I wish everyone was more like me." He goes to the coffee shop and the waitress there irritates him too, so he goes again, "I wish everyone was more like me." In his mind, they are all treating him wrong, and the world would be so much better if only they were all more like him.

The next morning he wakes up in the Twilight Zone, and everyone around him is him, just dressed in different clothes. Now the person at the concierge counter is exactly like him, the person next to him in the elevator is exactly like him, the waitress in the coffee shop is exactly like him, everyone at work is exactly like him. He is surrounded by himself the whole day, and by the end of it he exclaims, "God, I just want everyone to be the way they were."

There is a higher, balanced order in society. Ignorance is seeing one half and ignoring the other, while wisdom is seeing both sides of every event and of every person. In society, for every cruel person there is a kind one, and for every reprimand there is praise. If you are on the lookout for the balance, you will find it, and you will see divine perfection all around you and will feel that you are loved. There is ultimately nothing but love. There is a perfect balance of support and challenge, and you need both. The harsh side and the tough love make you independent, and the soft love makes you dependent. The two together make you whole. When you come to appreciate this wholeness, you experience the Gratitude Effect.

Woe to the man whose heart has not learned while young to hope, to love – and to put its trust in life.

– JOSEPH CONRAD

Our social life is not limited by groups we belong to, our work, our neighborhood, and our friends. Strangers are important too. I met a bum on a street of El Paso, Texas, who changed my life. He took me to the public library, showed me some amazing books written by Plato and Aristotle and taught me about the value of love and wisdom. That was a special stranger. Later another stranger found me in my tent in a jungle near a beach where I had been lying unconscious for three days nearly dying of poisoning. She stayed with me and cleaned up my tent as I began my healing. That was some stranger. I don't believe in necessarily staying away from strangers. My whole life as a teenager revolved around meeting strangers. I had a lot of rich experiences and a lot of great opportunities because of them. They helped me understand the Gratitude Effect.

Chance encounters, even if they last only two seconds, can change your life. When I bump into people, I usually don't say, "I'm sorry." I say, "Oh, hi. You were so attractive, I ran into you. What's your name?" Who is to say it was a mistake. We don't know.

Why Half the World Doesn't Like Me

Happiness (gratitude) is not a matter of intensity but of balance, order, rhythm and harmony.

– THOMAS MERTON

When you master the Gratitude Effect, you will realize that our worry and anxiety are only illusions. They stem from the assumptions that in the future we are going to experience more pain than pleasure, more loss than gain, more negativity than positivity, more challenge than support, and more turmoil than peace from someone or ourselves. In actuality, such an imbalance can't even occur. There is never someone challenging us without someone giving us support, and there is never someone criticizing us without someone praising us at the same time. There is always someone else to balance the imagined polarity. They may be close or distant, but they are always there. May I emphasize the word "imagined". It's the key here. We can never experience only one side to life. Life is perfectly balanced. That's why half the world won't like me – because the other half does. The Gratitude Effect involves embracing this amazing and heart opening balance.

Listen to these three amazing stories of balance from my life. In 1988 I got a Chiropractor of the Year Award. There was a big ceremony held partly in my honour, and my professional colleagues from around the world were acknowledging my achievement in front of thousands of people. At the same time, there were thousands of people with posters and flyers outside a large Baptist Church in Texas, saying that I was the anti-Christ himself. So, on the same day I was getting honoured by thousands of people, and I was also getting condemned by thousands of people. That's the balance of life. If you are not willing to be both honoured and crucified, it means you are not willing to fulfill your greatest purpose in life. No matter what you do, you will have both praise and reprimand. Be ready for both. The person who is most grateful is the person who is willing to embrace both and see that they are both necessary. If we get nothing but praise, we get puffed up and think we are bigger than we actually are. If we get nothing but criticism, we get pushed down lower than we are. When we get both, we get to be who we are.

This next experience of humbling balance happened in New York where I was speaking to a group of about a hundred and fifty people. After my talk, a nice gentleman came up to me and said, "I felt like I was in the presence of Socrates, Plato, Aristotle, Spinoza, or Emerson." He listed these five names of great philosophers that I admired, putting me in the same category with them. He was building me up and praising me. At that same moment, and I mean exactly the same (I checked the time later), I got an email from a professor who had read some of my books and thought they were just awful and utterly sick. In his letter he said, "You are no better than the Taliban, Jerry Falwell, George Bush, Hitler or Saddam Hussein." He was condemning me for being what he considered some kind of religious fundamentalist, and he listed five people he despised and put me in the same category with them. So I got five people in his email versus the five people from the person at my talk. I chuckled and said, "Thank you, universe, for being so magnificently balanced." That synchronicity was empowering, and it certainly initiated the Gratitude Effect.

The word 'happiness' would lose its meaning if it were not balanced by sadness.
– *CARL GUSTAV JUNG*

My third story of divine perfection takes us to South Africa. Recently, when I was in Johannesburg, some staff member broke into my hotel room and took about six thousand dollars.

Meanwhile, I was downstairs having business negotiations, and as a result, I was offered to speak at a conference. What do you think was the figure offered to me for this speaking engagement? You guessed it – it was neither more, nor less than six thousand dollars. I just laughed once I became aware of the synchronicity.

Many people want everyone around them to be peaceful and positive, supportive and kind. We become bi-polar by always trying to avoid people who challenge us and by being addicted to people who praise us. It's inevitably a futile game. What we don't realize is that if we are supported all the time, we don't grow. It is challenges that make us grow. Norman Vincent Peale once said, "If you ever wake up without a problem, get down on your hands and knees and pray for one, because you died."

The person who breaks free from this one-sided fantasy and sees the whole picture becomes grateful for each stage of the game, and comes out at the top as an empowered self-actualized individual. All those stages are parts of the equation, but the pinnacle of the equation is gratitude and love. The pinnacle brings out the Gratitude Effect.

Thank God for Bullies

Life's challenges are not supposed to paralyze you, they're supposed to help you discover who you are.
– *BERNICE JOHNSON REAGON*

I was presenting a speech in Houston, Texas, and there was a lady in the audience who was constantly asking questions. Every two minutes she would ask another question. It was starting to be a bit of a nuisance because I was trying to build a momentum in my speech but she would interrupt it with her next question. Instead of correcting the situation, I chose to ignore it because

I wanted to watch the class dynamic. I purposely let it go on just to see if someone would speak up. Whenever there is a dominating person, others will be quiet and not speak up. They will be repressing the questions they have inside, and what they wish to say.

She kept asking questions, and finally one lady stood up and said, "My God, would you shut your freaking mouth. We all paid to hear Dr. Demartini speak, instead we are listening to the dialogue between you two." So, this lady calmed down for about fifteen minutes. I went on speaking, and then she resumed her barrage of questions.

Somebody else said to her, "I thought we already discussed this," and so I finally said to the entire class, "If you are thinking about questions but not asking them because you are afraid to speak up, she will. She is expressing what others in the group are repressing. And she is not afraid to ask questions. If all of you asked a question every two minutes, she would calm down." It was a perfect demonstration of the principles of group dynamics at work. Compared to my other seminars, the average number of questions was the same, but this time instead of being diversified, almost all of the questions were coming from one person.

The same happens in our family dynamics and in our social environment. If there is a quiet person, there will also be an over-expressive person. Any area of your life that you don't express, other people are going to express for you. If you are afraid to be judged, if you are afraid to speak up, and go for what you love, you will end up working for someone else and will be told what to do.

I am grateful even for bullies because they are telling us to empower all areas of our life and to awaken to the inherent balance. Here is an example from my life. When I was a teenager, surfers and cowboys didn't get along too well. One day as I was walking down the street in El Paso, Texas, sporting my long hair and my surfboard, three cowboys lined up across the sidewalk blocking my way. I knew exactly what they had in mind. It was going to be a brawl.

I didn't know what to do at first. If I went inside the shop, I'd be trapped. If I went across the street, I'll get run over, and if I tried to run, I wouldn't be able to outrun them with my surfboard. I knew I had to go through this. And then my inner voice told me to... bark. I started barking and growling at these guys, and lo and behold, they moved aside. Instead of running or hiding, I confronted them, and they weren't expecting it. It was a pattern interruption for them to have a hippie surfer kid attacking them like a mad dog or a wolf. Those bullies helped me empower myself. Learning to face my fears was the benefit of being trapped. The bullies were guiding me to grow. Everything in that situation was something to be grateful for. I came out of it as surprised as they were, thinking, "Wow, I can take on situations like that and I can handle them." And during the biggest crisis there came one of the greatest blessings of my life. My mentor showed up, but that's another story.

Challenges are what makes life interesting;
overcoming them is what makes life meaningful.
– JOSHUA J. MARINE

When I was a teenager, I was bullied too. It made me work out and do bodybuilding, and nobody bothered me any more. When someone is bullying you, it means that you have disempowered some area of your life where you could excel. So, someone comes into your life and overpowers you in that area, be it physical, financial, or any other area.

There is another possible scenario. Maybe some people are bullying you on the playground because you are bullying them in class with your intelligence. They can't keep up with you and feel beaten up because you are getting all the attention and all the grades, and they are not. So, you may be beating them up without realizing it. If you don't empower certain areas of your life, life makes sure that some place along the way, you get kicked in the butt to finally wake up and empower it.

When people get bullied and pushed, it also means that they have someone who is not disciplining them enough. If the parents are not doing it, the police will do it. If the parents are overprotective, a bully comes along to beat them up. When I was about six years old, there was a kid who lived around the corner. He had some sort of immunity problem. I was too young to know exactly what it was, but it was some health issue. His parents were overprotective of him – they didn't want him outside, and they never let him play in the sun. As a result, he was ostracized by everybody. Kids would push him; they would ride their bicycles by him and kick him or knock his books down. They were bullying him constantly. The more his parents tried to protect him, the more other kids tried to set him free from this protection. The violent bullies were there to balance out the overprotective parents. In life, when you have the one, you get the other. And seeing the two together is the key to understanding. Gratitude is a balanced perspective. It is not just the one supportive side that helps you. The challenge is a part of the big picture too. I am grateful for both sides of the coin of life.

When things seem to be supportive and going our way, we say, "Oh, thank you, thank you, thank you." When things seem to be challenging and going against our values, we go, "Oh damn it, damn it, damn it." When there is a balance of support and challenge simultaneously, we say, "Thank you," and we become truly grateful. The normally hidden divine order reveals itself. This is truly the Gratitude Effect.

There are Two Tellings to Every Story

There are no mistakes, no coincidences. All events are blessings given to us to learn from.
– *ELIZABETH KÜBLER-ROSS*

When we can train ourselves to recognize this hidden order and balance of things, we will see clearly that there is no such thing as a negative event. There's no such thing as a purely positive event either. There's just an event. All events are neutral until we judge and label them. For example, if it rains, a farmer is grateful because the rain brings relief from the drought, but a beautiful bride is heartbroken because the rain has ruined the most important day in her life. The rain is neither good nor bad, but if we don't like when it's happening, we hate it. If we've been waiting for it, we praise heavens for answering our prayers. Understanding this will allow you to see that if you are hurt by any situation, you haven't found its benefits yet, and you have to keep looking until you find the true and inherent balance with its accompanying gratitude in your heart.

The recent tsunami in South East Asia had just as many benefits as it had drawbacks. But sensation, anxiety and fear sell, so media capitalizes on this, and that's why we don't hear about the benefits. I started collecting them right after the tsunami occurred. For example, as we know, the area was completely washed over, but when the water finally subsided, the corn grew faster than ever and was full of nutrients. The bicycle business was booming, so was the construction business, and there were people saying, "Thank God, this occurred. This is the best thing that could happen." Some people were down, and some people were up. We only hear about the negative side of the story. We hear of the devastation. But as an Irish proverb says, there are two tellings to every story.

The greatest relief effort in the world emerged out of this tragedy. Thousands of people who were just sitting on their butt without having a cause in life, now awakened to a greater cause. They became motivated and inspired to do something in the world. They found out they were capable of doing things they had never dreamed of.

I refuse to see a crisis without blessing. Just because people label something terrible, doesn't mean it really is. It simply means that they haven't taken the time to look deep enough to see the hidden terrific. It doesn't mean we don't have to respond to these so-called "disasters" or emergencies. People who react in situations like this will go on to rescue the survivors and solve the apparent and immediate "problem". It's important and valuable, but we don't want to forget the other side too. If you see both sides, you don't react, you wisely act. There is an astounding difference.

Every Cloud has a Silver Lining, or Another Look at 9/11

Everything that is, is freely given by the God of love. All is grace. Light and water, shelter and food, work and free time, children, parents, grandparents, life and death – it is all given to us. Why? So that we can say thanks: thanks to God, thanks to each other, thanks to all and everyone.

– HENRI NOUWEN

On September eleventh of 2001, I was on the plane that was landing in Sydney, Australia. Suddenly there came an announcement from the flight captain over the public address system about the New York – World Trade Center and the Washington – Pentagon. My first reaction was one of suspense and intrigue. When I got into the transit Qantas Club Lounge at the Sydney airport along with hundreds of other travelers, we all watched the re-plays of the crashing explosions on the TV monitors. Because the international telephones were flooded, I was unable to communicate with the U.S. for a couple of days. My beautiful wife Athena was in our residence at Trump Tower in New York City when these events occurred, but she was not injured though shocked and certainly concerned.

Because I had a delay before my flight to Perth, Australia, I had a moment to reflect on what was happening, and I began writing an initial list of blessings concerning this world-changing event. My computer was frozen, the batteries were down and I forgot to place an Australian adapter in my carry case, so I wrote these blessings on an envelope.

At first glance this pre-meditated event may seem to be loss without gain, war without peace, death without life, darkness without light, and destruction without construction. But this is not the whole truth; for, there are no crises without blessings. Some of the blessings are so profound that only an event of such magnitude could have initiated them. Below are a few transcriptions of the many blessings from my envelope:

- Unification within U.S. families
- Stronger mutual appreciation within American families
- Worldwide unification of individuals in display of solidarity
- New York City reconstruction and transformation
- Increased acts of heroic courage balancing out the acts of the so-called "cowardly villains"
- Reduced numbers of homicides and suicides due to angry or depressed people being drawn to causes outside themselves
- Reduced N.Y.C. traffic and traffic casualties
- Reduced domestic violence due to the outwardly expressed repressions of inner turmoil, anger and tension
- Reduced divorce rates
- Reduced number of family quarrels

- Increased lovemaking and increased birth rate resulting from people stranded at home, loving and appreciating each other
- Global unification to compensate for the intense moment of local division
- Global prayer
- Global hugging
- Global kindness
- Increased global conversations and discussions
- Increased global peaceful meditation and silence
- Global outpouring of heartfelt love
- Global appreciation for America
- Global religious services
- Greater appreciation for the military (Marines, Navy...)
- Greater appreciation for the FBI and CIA
- Greater appreciation for the fire fighters
- Greater appreciation for the police
- Greater appreciation for the National Guard
- Greater appreciation for the civic service organizations
- Greater appreciation for the Red Cross
- Greater appreciation and business for the rescue crews
- Greater appreciation and business for the ambulance transportation services
- Greater appreciation and business for the emergency medical services
- Greater appreciation and business for the emergency equipment services
- Greater appreciation and business for the hospitals
- Greater appreciation and business for the demolition and clean up crews
- Greater global security procedures
- Greater air traffic control monitoring
- Greater understanding of 'terrorism'
- Greater display of U.S. patriotism (increased display of

American flag)
- Greater exploration and understanding of other countries' values and needs
- Wake up call to the reality of America's vulnerability – Humbling U.S. resulting in deep self-reflection and self-inspection
- Correction of overvalued real estate prices
- Correction and then soon significant rebound of U.S. financial markets
- Correction of overvalued airline prices
- Increased quality airline service
- Correction of overvalued hotel prices
- Increased cell phone, and telephone telecommunication uses
- Increased television and radio communication viewing and listening
- Increased book, magazine, newspaper and tabloid printing and distribution
- Increased N.Y.C. sales of respiratory devices
- Increased N.Y.C. business for funeral service industry – burials and memorial services
- Increased business for N.Y.C. flower growing industry
- Increased business for N.Y.C. casket industry
- Increased business for N.Y.C. steel manufacturing industry
- Increased business for N.Y.C. cement industry
- Increased business for N.Y.C. glass industry
- Increased business for N.Y.C. waste management services industry
- Increased business for tree farming and wood industry
- Increased business for greetings card industry
- Increased business for N.Y.C. architectural industry
- Increased architectural engineering awareness and revised building restrictions
- Increased number of alternative U.S. transportation means

- Increased dedication to world causes
- Increased understanding of human psychology
- Increased business for the psychological or psychiatric service industry
- Increased business for the pharmacological industry
- A moment in history that the whole world will remember
- The future making of the most viewed movie on earth
- Future world-renowned and historical N.Y. memorial and increased tourism
- National holiday – vacation
- Greater value of the Demartini Method® of stress reduction…

There is suffering in heaven, for where there is the capacity for pleasure there is the capacity for pain.
– *WILLIAM BLAKE*

The list doesn't have to stop there, but I think I have made my point. Every event has two sides. Accompanying every crisis is a blessing, and during every moment of turmoil, there is an accompanying and refreshing calm. That's why I do not to see the events of September eleventh as purely destructive. I see them as transformative. They simply offered me an opportunity to see God (the Grand Organized Design) working in action, for the will of God is equilibrium.

On one hand there is destruction and war and yet on the other there is reconstruction and peace. Division and unity, separation and togetherness, kindness and cruelty are walking hand in hand. It is as if the divine universal laws intended such a humbling balance. We may be fooled if we look too quickly. So let us look again, and this time let us look deeper. Out of every great challenge comes a greater opportunity. What will it take for us to see the big picture? Isn't life a perfect masterpiece? May we look through out hearts and open our eyes to the gift of balance that lies before us. May we humble our opinions before the majesty of the Grand Organized Design.

What's That in Your Eye?

If we see a speck in a brother's eye, we must first see if there is a log in our own eye; perhaps that speck in our brother's eye is only a reflection of the beam in our own.
– *DAVID WATSON*

If you live in America, you will hear predominantly one side of the September eleventh events – you will see them as terrible and unprovoked. You will also possibly consider the radical group of Afghans as evil. But obviously the individuals slamming into the World Trade Center and their supporters considered this event as good, and perceived the Americans as evil. They celebrated this event as 'terrific' and thought it was a retribution for America's previous evil doing.

As I have traveled the globe, I have heard both sides of these September events from people in different countries. Many people I talked to had mixed or negative feelings about the American way of life, or "greedy capitalistic, resource consuming system" as some of them have called it. Many Europeans have distaste for the American's dominating and terrorizing ways and means. I see both sides and can say thank you for both views as they hone my mind in on the equilibrating truth. There is a part of the whole truth in both camps. Both camps have a light and a shadow side.

We must look deeply at ourselves before we react irrationally to these life-changing events because what we are reacting to is but a reflection of what we have yet to love within ourselves. We attract into our living experiences our disowned parts, individually as well as socially. We make more of a difference when we love than when we attempt to retaliate through brute force. What we try to change in others only resists us. What we love in others turns around and assists us. Our enemy is eternally ourselves. May we awaken to the power of the Gratitude Effect.

A loving person lives in a loving world. A hostile person lives in a hostile world. Everyone you meet is your mirror.
– KEN KEYS

The U.S. is now facing its own shadow. Yet it is resorting to the very tactics it once condemned. What we say we would never do is what we attract. What we condemn we breed or become. We are here to learn love and be appreciative, and God has many ways of teaching us grace.

Every time we point a finger at someone, there are three fingers pointing back. If we get a strong reaction to any culture, religion, subculture, or a smaller social group, we haven't learnt to love parts of ourselves. They are just a reflection of us. When we see someone we admire, we tend to look up to them and humbly disown the admirable traits inside ourselves. When we see someone we despise, we tend to look down on them and proudly disown the despicable traits inside ourselves. Yet there the traits lie buried from our initial view. It takes honest evaluation to discover them, but in doing so we are set free to love these traits in others and ourselves. Traits are not to become eliminated or condemned, only understood and loved.

What we perceive in others lies within ourselves. Everyone is truly our mirror. The seer, the seeing, and the seen are the same. The outer world reflects our inner selves. At first, our minds want to disown what we see. But a deeper look will reveal the truth.

How Could You Do This to Me!

We don't know who we are until we see what we can do.
– MARTHA GRIMES

More often than not the issue that divides people into opposing camps and makes them clash is power struggle. Having too much power is just as challenging as having too little. In the family dynamic, people who are only focused on their spiritual and family goals, and only want peace, are more likely to attract violent people. Those who don't have an education, a job, or money, and are not socially connected or don't have the ability to fight back are more likely to get violently beaten. This situation is meant to make them stand up and grow. They have to become strong and decide what they want. Any area of our life that we don't empower, someone else is going to overpower.

The same with cultures – when a culture is disempowered in seven areas of life – when the great majority of its people have a spiritual quest and a family devotion, but don't have a great mind development through education, they are not making a business contribution to the world, they don't have much money per capita, they don't have advanced social interactions or networking with other countries, they are isolated, and they don't have strong military or adequate health care system, they are highly likely to become overrun by dictators. Dictators are not evil people. They are a by-product of a disempowered culture. People always talk about Hitler killing six million Jews, but I doubt it that one man actually went out and killed six million people himself. He made orders, and thousands of people obeyed him, went and killed six million people.

People often have misperceptions of history, and much of history writing is biased. If we learnt to recognize both sides of any event, we would transform and adjust our misperceptions. Whenever a culture rises up and its people think they are the ones, the chosen ones, the unique and the right ones, and everyone else are wrong, they generally find themselves getting attacked. This pattern has occurred throughout history for centuries. That's what is going on in certain cultures even today. They are constantly getting attacked because they think they are the chosen ones. The Australians call it the tall poppy syndrome – for the tall poppies are the ones that get cut down. Self-righteous people who think they are special, unique, and misunderstood get attacked more than others. It's called pride before the fall.

A while ago I had a chance to do some counselling work with a twenty-something-year-old girl in South Africa whose boyfriend was an Al-Qaeda member. She was frightened of him to the point of demonstrating schizophrenic signs. Apparently they were both a bit bi-polar. It was a perfect match. When I was working with her, it was a bit risky. She was concerned that he would kill her, especially if he found out that she talked to me about him.

As we worked on her perceptions of the whole victim-aggressor situation, her power came back. Her confidence did too. Being disempowered, she attracted this type of person. As would be expected according to the inherent balance, she was also surrounded by people who supported her and wanted to protect her, and this person was trying to challenge her. She had to integrate both sides. And when she did, it changed her life. She stood up to him and said, "I am not going to date you. If you have to kill me, that's okay." She went out about her life and never had a problem with him again. It was the state of her own certainty that made a difference.

I watch this happen regularly with domestic violence victims. I get attacked a lot for this belief, but I truly believe that the so-called disempowered "victims" are a part of the single equation. Disempowered people are attracting their circumstances. People who are empowered don't have or attract the same experiences. The Gratitude Effect can empower you and disarm others.

We often give our enemies the means to our own destruction.
– AESOP

Victim mentality is assuming that somebody has done something to us. I don't completely buy this. If you don't believe me, come and attend one of my seminars entitled the Breakthrough Experience where you will personally experience the Demartini Method® of dissolving the victim-violator mentality. The very first question I will ask you will be, "What have they done to you that is so terrible? And then I will ask you, "Where have you done the same thing in some way?" You will own every single trait you despise, because they are all in you and they all serve. Every single one of them, without exception. You will see that there is no one to forgive, but there is the whole world to love.

A couple of years ago I worked with a lady from High Valley Ranch in California who had been hit over the head with a bottle, stabbed eighteen times and...An hour into our session, utilizing the Demartini Method®, we saw the assumed pain transform into profound gratitude and love. She saw the order in what had happened to her, and she became grateful for it. She was no longer a victim. She went on to do a radio show with me and shared her story with thousands if not millions of people. She was able to get focused again and turn her life around.

It is not truly what happens to you that matters. What matters is how you perceive what happens. I've seen incest, I've seen murder, I've seen rape, and I've seen it dissolve into love and gratitude with the power of the Demartini Method and its by-product, the Gratitude Effect. It is truly inspiring to see this happen. I have accomplished this result tens of thousands of times. If you would love to transform your blame, guilt, or shame into gratitude, then find your way to the Breakthrough Experience®. There is no reason to carry around a victim mentality any longer because it is neither going to empower your life nor is it going to let you grow. When we believe an illusion, it takes courage to discover the truth.

S.O.S. My Reality Wouldn't Fit into My Fantasy

We must learn to tailor our concepts to fit reality, instead of trying to stuff reality into our concepts.
– *VICTOR DANIELS*

Why can't we be happy all the time? The answer is simple – because the one sided mask called happiness by itself is a fantasy and an illusion. The addiction to this one tiny illusion gives rise to a whole realm of social concerns – stress, heartache, hopelessness, anger, resentment, blame, depression and even suicide! There are twelve major fantasies or delusions that people often live with, and those fantasies are major obstacles on the path to gratitude and are ultimately a cause of our nightmares. How can we be grateful for life when in our fantasy world we know exactly how life is supposed to be? I am going to let you in on a big secret. Life is the way it is. If we want it to correspond to our fantasies, we are setting ourselves up for self-defeat, anger, frustration, negativity and ingratitude.

The first fantasy is expecting others to live outside of the universal laws. Sometimes we expect only half of our partner, spouse, friends, sister, neighbor, classmate, or a stranger. We want people always to be nice without ever being mean, always kind without ever being cruel, cooperative without ever being competitive, etc. We only want the "good stuff". Expecting people to be one-sided beings is like expecting to find a one-sided magnet. Have you ever seen one?

The second fantasy is expecting others to be living outside of their values. If we expect them to abandon their values and live according to ours, we are guaranteed disappointment and frustration. Anger is nothing but a projection of our own values onto someone and expecting them to prefer our values to their own.

The third fantasy is the combination of the first two. It manifests when we want people to be someone they can't be because it's against the laws of the universe and outside of their values.

The same applies to us. If we expect ourselves to live outside of the universal laws, we are trying to live out fantasy number four. We want only to be happy, never sad; only supportive, never challenging; always positive, never negative. But we cannot be living someone else's values either, and to expect that of ourselves is another fantasy. The last two fantasies combined produce an even bigger fantasy. That's number six. And, the next big fantasy, drum roll please, is to be doing it to others and ourselves simultaneously. That's all of the above fantasies together. How can we have gratitude for the world or for ourselves if we are trying to change everything and everyone?

The eighth and ninth fantasies are the unrealistic expectations on what we imagine God to be (often some anthropomorphic projection of our mortal selves); and to live outside the laws of the universe and to live outside our own projected human values. The tenth fantasy is the combination of the eighth and ninth delusions.

The eleventh and twelfth fantasies are the unrealistic expectations of mechanical objects to defy the laws of physics that govern them, and to perform in any manner other than that for which they were designed.

Reality doesn't bite, rather our perception of reality bites.
– ANTHONY J D'ANGELO

The greatest discovery is that we have the power to alter our sensory perceptions and our motor functions. It means that we can change the way we perceive our world, or we can change the way we act on it. If we are dissatisfied with how things are going in our life, we always have these two options. If nothing else, when it seems like our life is going in the opposite direction from our goals and dreams, at least it is giving us feedback to correct our perceptions or course. Setting our goals according to the universal laws and our values is the wisest way to take control over our destiny and to transform our world. I am convinced that we cannot achieve fulfillment by running away from half of our life into the world of fantasies where everyone is always nice and looks like a supermodel, where there's perpetual honeymoon and no stress. These fantasies are the very source of our mental suffering and depression. I personally gave up happiness because it made me too sad. I prefer the true and balanced power of the Gratitude Effect.

> *The reality of life is that your perceptions – right or wrong – influence everything else you do. When you get a proper perspective of your perceptions, you may be surprised how many other things fall into place.*
>
> – *ROGER BIRKMAN*

Questions to Offer You a Gift of New Vision

- Everyone is a leader in some area. Where would you love to lead?
- What aspects of nature and society can you be grateful for?
- Where would you love to go?
- What would you love to do socially?
- Who would you love to meet?
- How is the person who appears to be your enemy actually serving you?

- How is a cultural or religious belief that you don't appreciate serving the world?
- How can you be grateful for someone who has a completely different religious system?
- How can you be grateful for someone with a completely different value system?
- How do they serve the world?
- How can you be grateful for what appears to be loss and destruction in the world? How do they serve the world?

Affirmations of Appreciation

No matter who you are, you are worthy of love. I love you just the way you are.
No matter what creed, race, sex, colour, age, or religion you are, you are a reflection of me, and I love you.
No matter how wealthy or poor you are, you are a reflection of me, and I love you.
You serve the world by being exactly who you are.
Thank you for being rich.
Thank you for being poor.
Thank you for being overweight.
Thank you for being thin.
Thank you for being dark.
Thank you for being white.
Did you get the idea? Continue the appreciation list in your head.

Practise Transforming Your Perceptions of the World

Exercise 1. Find something that's happening in the world that you think is terrible. Choose something that really pushes your buttons. Find the opposite side of it and write down how it serves. Find as many positive things as you need until you see that it is just an event. It's neutral and has both sides to be grateful for. Analyze it from both perspectives and work on it until you feel gratitude. Otherwise it will run your life. How can this event be of service to you, your loved ones and to the world?

Exercise 2. What is it in your life that you never said thank you for? Scan your life. Go back to your childhood. Choose an event, and ask:

- How does it serve my mission in life?
- How does it serve me in the spiritual area?
- How does it serve me in my mental life?
- How does it serve me in the financial area of my life?
- How does it serve me in my vocational area?
- How does it serve me in my family life?
- How does it serve me in my social life?
- How does it serve me in the physical area of my life?
- How does it serve others and the world?

Exercise 3. Make an effort to be adaptable and open to new people coming into your life, and go out of your way to develop communications that will enrich your and their lives. This may mean that you don't wait for others to invite you somewhere; but you take the initiative and organize get-togethers yourself. Each day make an effort to expand your social network and communications and explore new possibilities for yourself. Making a phone call or sending a card to someone you would love to have as a colleague or taking time for new acquaintances can set all kinds of new social wheels spinning.

CHAPTER 8

Healing with Gratitude

What If You Were Already Perfect?

Take care of your body. It's the only place you have to live.
– *JIM ROHN*

The greatest art form that exists on this planet is the human body. What a magnificently structured temple of sacred architecture our body is. Are we grateful for it? Some are, but most take this wonderful gift for granted. Many complain about the shape of their body – I'm too fat, too thin, too short, or too tall. They spend a great deal of time in front of the mirror focusing on what they perceive as imperfections of their body, rather than focusing on its magnificently balanced perfection.

When we look in the mirror, all of us will have things we like and dislike about physical structures. Working with thousands of people, I became convinced that for every part of our body we don't like, there is a part we admire. If we are putting ourselves down in one area, I guarantee, we are being proud of another area. We may not like our thighs, but we will admire our eyes. We may not like our thin hair, but we will admire our skin. We may not like the shape of our body, but we will like the shape of our lips and our smile, and so on.

One of the reasons why some people beat themselves up about certain areas of their bodies is because they are comparing themselves to a fantasy of some magazine cover that they think they are supposed to look like. We need that area to keep us humble and to keep us growing. If we only had things we liked about ourselves, we would get puffed up and overly proud and alienate ourselves from other loving and lovable people. Have you ever met people who thought they were all that – the people who were marvelous in every area, and didn't need to grow or evolve anymore? That's right, you probably wanted to get away from them as soon as possible. If we ever feel we are done, we may not relate to other people and may isolate ourselves. On the other hand, if we only had things we disliked, we would be too humble to be around people.

I worked with a lovely lady who you might not necessarily call classically beautiful, but she loved her hair, thought her eyebrows were wonderful and her teeth were perfect. She had the smoothest skin because she had never gone out to the beach when everyone else did. So, now at forty-five she had baby-smooth skin while everyone else who lived in the sun had burned skin with age spots on it. She told me, "I love my skin. When a man touches my skin, it feels so smooth."

I worked with a supermodel in Canada who, I thought, was beautiful from head to toe but she didn't think so. She focused on exactly half of her body she didn't like. What's not to like? Well, she thought one of her eyes was off to one side if you looked from a certain angle, her breasts weren't balanced, one of her eyebrows was plucked too much and was too thin, one of her teeth was crooked, or so she thought, her hair was always folding on one side… Well, you get my point. Her body had the balance of things she liked and disliked, and so does everybody else's.

No matter who you are, you have things you like and dislike, or even admire and despise about yourself. Everyone practises the same math: fifty-fifty, right down the middle. But both things you like and dislike are going to serve you in your life, and the wisdom is appreciating this balance and being grateful for it. The Gratitude Effect also encompasses your beautifully balanced body. To love it is to appreciate what is assumed to be attractive and repulsive.

Perfection is another name for reality.
– *BARUCH SPINOZA*

Our physical body is truly magnificent. It is an amazing marvel, designed in accordance with the principles that govern all energy and matter. Our senses conclude that our physical body is solid, but our entire body is actually made up of many components, the smallest of which are waves and particles in perpetual motion.

Let's take a quick look at our physical construction. Our body can be divided into systems, such as the nervous system, cardiovascular system, genitourinary system, muscular system, etc. These systems are made up of organs, e,g., heart, brain, stomach, liver, and so on. Our organs are made up of tissues that are made up of cells. The cells are made of molecules, and molecules are made of atoms. The billions of atoms that make up our body are composed of subatomic particles.

According to quantum physics, every subatomic particle can be described in terms of waves. The protons, electrons, and neutrons in the atoms of our cells and the smaller particles in the nucleus of these atoms are all waves. Our entire body is made up of electro-magnetically resonant waves and particles, or light.

Deep inside the subtle vibrations of the atoms of our body, the subatomic particles are vibrating at trillions upon trillions of cycles per second. The building blocks that comprise our body are trilling with magnificent energy. At the most fundamental level, we are vibrating wave phenomena, harmonized and in perfect balance. This has profound significance because it indicates that the universal principles that govern light waves, also govern us.

Ultimately, we are truly brilliant and enlightened human beings maintaining a hidden order. We are vibrating with and attuning to different levels of energy vibrations or waves, from very low to very high frequencies. We resonate with and relate to all of the frequencies in existence from the subatomic to the astronomical wavelengths. In fact, we are constantly being bombarded by waves and particles of all different frequencies whether we are aware of it or not. When you consciously choose to attune your mind to higher frequency thoughts and ideas, your understanding and appreciation for your balanced perfection increases exponentially, and you come to rediscover your own magnificence. Being grateful for your body and for the multitude of its powerful gifts can make the difference between experiencing wellness or illness. With the Gratitude Effect we enliven our form.

Your Body Is a Gift

Life is the first gift, love is the second, and understanding the third.

– *MARGE PIERCY*

When I encourage you to be grateful for your body, I mean the whole body as it is. Some people will find it hard to be grateful if they or someone in their family was born with some disability or deformity, but I am convinced that everyone receives an advantage no matter what you were born with or have gone through. And the so-called disability is a gift too.

I had a young girl patient who was brain damaged. She salivated and laughed most of the time. I never saw her cry. Her family was expressing her sorrow, but she was laughing most of the time. They would go, "My God, how can she be so playful and happy all the time?" She was so-called mentally challenged, and it looked like that's all she ever did – laugh and play. She seemed incapable of experiencing negative emotions at all. Is this not a balancing gift to the family?

I also worked with a young lady who had polio, and her legs were really small; in fact, she hardly had any. But she attracted as a husband this giant guy about six foot six and nearly three hundred pounds that carried her around all the time. He would literally hold her on his arm and they would go places together, and everyone thought, "Wow, what a beautiful couple." The universe brought those two together in this unexpected display of love. In conventional terms, she had a deformed body, but she had beautiful eyes, beautiful hair, beautiful face, beautiful smile and beautiful manners. Nature always provides some advantage to everyone. Just keep looking.

I was also born with some physical deformities. My foot and my hand were turned in, and I had to wear braces. I really wanted to run and to straighten my leg. When I was a little kid, I would go down to the corner and wait for my dad to come home at six o'clock so I could race him back down the street just to show him that I could run straight.

I also wanted to play baseball. Legally, at seven, I was not supposed to play baseball; I had to be eight. But I begged the coaches on the Pee-Wee League to let me play and be the batboy because I could run, get the bat and run back, and I could show off my running. I really was determined to run. They let me practise, play and run with older kids, and it meant everything to me. They would hit the ball and drop the bat, and I would run and get it. It made me feel like I was doing something important in baseball. I was very grateful for the opportunity to get the bat.

When I was eight years old, I got to play in the Little League, and when I turned ten, my coaches broke the rules and let me play in the All Star game with eleven-, and twelve-year-old kids. I was the only one who got to do that, and I believe it was because I was so grateful for the opportunity to run, and I did the extra work and went the extra mile. I ran harder, I pitched longer, I caught more, I batted more, I practised more than anybody because I wanted to play more than anybody else, and I was so grateful that I could play that they gave me more opportunities. Eventually I got to be the pitcher of the Little League All Stars, even though I wasn't even in the proper age group. I was called the Strikeout King because I was one of the most consistent pitchers they had. My point is that the Gratitude Effect allowed me to get advances and promotions that I wouldn't have gotten otherwise. I was not able to shine in academics, but I was able to excel in sports, and, for that, I was grateful. I guess, early on, I intuitively made the Gratitude Effect a part of my life.

Let's Search for Hidden Motives, or Everyone Loves a Detective Story

Our bodies are our gardens – our wills are our gardeners.

– *WILLIAM SHAKESPEARE*

So many people conscientiously seem to go out of their way to break down this magnificent structure of their body by smoking, eating unhealthy foods, and not exercising. Many of them are not aware of their own hidden agendas that are leading them into potential illness. For example, when I work with people who are obese, I inevitably find unconscious motives there. It can be hundreds of things.

One of my clients has, in her mind, translated eating into a ritual of receiving love because when she was a child, she used to sit on her dad's lap and he used to feed her like that. This was the only time that she felt love from her dad. Unconsciously she continued to eat because she had associated food with her dad's love. Upon utilizing the Demartini Method® of emotional resolution on this and a few other related issues, she began reducing her weight.

Another female client of mine used to be very skinny and attractive, but because her husband was very busy and didn't give her enough attention, she received her attention from someone else, and she had an affair. She almost got caught and then regretted it very much. Right away she cut her hair and gained a lot of weight, basically making sure she wasn't as attractive because she didn't trust herself with other men and didn't want to jeopardize her family and security.

In another case, I worked with a large woman in Miami who didn't like her body at all and thought she was thirty to forty pounds overweight. When people are overweight, there is often a hidden motive behind it. So I asked her, "What are the benefits to your being overweight?" At first, she was shocked by my question, but slowly she became conscious of some hidden reasons she hadn't been aware of before. Here's what we discovered.

She was a lawyer, and when she first started her practice, she was very slim and attractive. But many of her clients were men, and their wives felt threatened by her beauty and made sure their husbands stopped doing any business with her. The second she realized that, she unconsciously put on weight, put on glasses and tried to do everything possible to make herself less attractive or threatening in order to keep the business.

At first, it was a subtle thing. But when I brought it to her attention, she realized that her extra weight was there on purpose. It helped her provide for her family, build her career, etc. She saw many reasons to be grateful for it. After she saw the purpose it served, we came up with alternative ways for her not to be threatening and still have her attractive body too. As soon as we did, she dropped some weight. It was all in her mind.

A while ago I worked with a doctor in California who had injured his back. His first reaction was devastation. It was going to be the end of his practice. The truth is he was burned out and was unconsciously thinking, "I don't know if I will be able to continue with my practice much longer." When he got injured, he learnt how to hire doctors, delegate things, and set up management structures. Now he has a practice that is much bigger than his previous one. He has other doctors working for him, while he is receiving percentages; and he is more efficient than ever. He looks back and says, "Thank God I had that injury, or I would never have become a multimillionaire."

Recently I worked with a lady who had cancer. I asked her to write down two hundred benefits of her illness, and as she did, she saw the other side of her disease, and she had tears of gratitude streaming down her cheeks. She said, "I had no idea how many benefits are coming out of this. It brought the family together again, it made me take time for myself, it taught me to delegate things and prioritize things. It made me realize how useful I was. It opened my eyes to what's important in life. I saw that people really cared about me. I learnt to say things that I could never say before. I realized how much energy I spent judging trivial things." She realized that a lot of things happened in her life that would never have happened had it not been for her cancer. She had an unconscious motive for it with secondary gains. Sometimes people are manifesting disease to get what they want without realizing they are doing it. So be aware of what you wish for, and be selectively strategic on how you would love it to manifest, it might just come true.

Accidents, and How We Attract Them

Your body is a temple, but only if you treat it as one.
– *ASTRID ALAUDA*

There are two types of healers: when we are depressed, comedy can act as a healer, but when we are manic, infatuated or elated, tragedy can act as a healer. Injury means jury from within, so when we are attracting an injury into our life along with the so-called trauma and tragedy, it could mean we are simply manic in some area of our life and are becoming readjusted on our course. Some time ago, a CEO of a major corporation came into my office in Houston for a consultation. He had two aeroplane crashes in one year, and he barely survived this last one.

I asked him, "Tell me about the moment the plane engine failed before the crash. What exactly was going on? Were you in anyway excited, elated or manic?"

He said, "Funny you should say this, but we were actually celebrating and we popped the champagne cork at the moment the engine malfunctioned. We were in the back of our private jet. I just closed a forty-million-dollar deal, so I put eleven million dollars in my pocket, popped the champagne and said to the pilot, 'Take it to the limit.' And as he did, the engine blew out."

He was manic, and he was exaggerating himself, and puffing himself up, and he attracted the humbling circumstance – pride before the fall.

"What about the other crash?"

"Yeah, it was after another deal. We were ecstatic."

If you still doubt that we attract accidents and trauma into our life, this next story will possibly persuade you a bit further. When I was a practicing chiropractor, I used to watch the patterns of injuries occurring amongst people who were having multiple accidents in short periods of time. I had a patient who had four car accidents in one year. This reoccurring theme awakened me to an underlying pattern and motive to this patient's injuries. I mean, come on, how could you have four of them in a row? But I figured it out, and here is how she did it.

She created them by living in her fantasy world. In her mind, her parents honoured her sister who was an overachiever more than her, and she felt like she could seldom get their attention. She felt she was the "screw-up" in the family. But when she got in a car accident, her parents came to her and gave her special attention. Even the sister came. She also received money for the accident. She was getting all these things, and the very day I told her that her spine was recovered and that she was now ready to be weaned back from her steady chiropractic care, she had another accident that very afternoon, and she came right back.

This happened four times in a row the second I released her. Then I realized that she had an unconscious motive for manifesting such accidents in her life. As long as she believed that they would bring her closer to her parents and would generally make her more of the centre of attention, she was going to go from one accident to another.

After four accidents I finally told her parents, "I am not going to treat your daughter any more unless there are some new approaches to recovery implemented. She is possibly going to destroy her body permanently the way she is headed, and I am not going to help her potentially do that. She is becoming dependent on creating accidents for economic reasons and for parental attention. Maybe it would be wise to let her know in a new way how much you love her and express it in ways other than primarily during injury recoveries. Ultimately, it is not wise to continue rescuing and rewarding her desperation and injury pattern. I would suggest that you concentrate on acknowledging her for her values and her greatest strengths in the areas she chooses to pursue. She feels that you have been honouring her sister's academic and business accomplishments, but you haven't honoured her own creativity and her other social and artistic talents. She feels that you have indirectly and unconsciously shown disappointment in her, and are making the other daughter a hero." After they recognized the motives underlying their daughter's dynamic, they became more attentive and supportive of her unique talents, and as a result, their daughter's image and her self-worth stabilized. The next year she had only one minor accident, and that was the last since. She also stabilized herself with a career that provided moderate, yet self-sustaining income.

She was attracting trauma into her life only as a strategy to get more attention from her family. When she didn't need to do it anymore, she stopped using this unconsciously motivated strategy.

There is little point in treating physical symptoms if the inner cause of illness or injury remains intact and the unconscious motives are not understood and dissolved. If you share your symptoms with a medical doctor, he might say, "You need some form of medication to balance them out." If you go to a naturopath, he might tell you, "You need a herb to balance them out." If you go to a chiropractor, he might say, "You need an adjustment to balance them out." If you go to a nutritionist, you might hear, "You need to take a nutritional supplement to balance them out."

All these experts have a special method of how they are going to bring balance back into your body. But still the most self-empowering and possibly the most efficient method of all is the Gratitude Effect, which is derived from mastering your own perceptions and harnessing the power from within your grateful mind. If you can awaken to the inherent balance existing within your mind, it will have the greatest impact on your body. And it is your mind that you have full command over. If you want control over your life, awaken to the true and ever present grateful balance, and you will regain command of your body. This does not mean excluding the various healing methods. It just means working in conjunction with the power of your mind. Most people don't want to be held accountable for their health issues, so they seek help from someone else. They want someone else to take care of it for them, but a mind that is balanced with gratitude and love for your life and for your body is still the greatest healer.

Don't You Ever Listen?

Our own physical body possesses a wisdom which we who inhabit the body lack. We give it orders which make no sense.

– HENRY MILLER

Wellness includes both concepts labeled as health and disease. If you eat a whole pizza at night and feel terrible the next day, are the morning symptoms you experience a form of disease, or is this your body guiding you to health? Some physicians may think it's a disease called indigestion, but a chiropractor or naturopath may say that it's your body trying to tell you to quit eating too much. So which is it? Both health and disease serve you depending on your interpretation, and I see a reason to be grateful for both.

There is no doubt our body is creating symptoms to give us feedback on how close or far we are from the balanced state of gratitude and love. When people are holding on to unrealistic expectations, or delusions which can result in hate or anger, they can run their immune system down. It's a well-known fact that cancer is often connected to anger, loss, high stress, etc. Any time we bring about a grateful balance to our perceptions, we bring about wholeness and well-being.

The Gratitude Effect brings physiological ease, order and wellness. It rallies our immune system and brings balance to the nervous system. It makes our cells work, the water molecules vibrate, and our whole body function optimally again. I believe that gratitude and love are the greatest healers. When we come to a point of gratitude, we release our pent up tensions and compressions in our body. We sleep differently. When our perceptions are ungratefully lopsided, our bodies create signs and symptoms to get us back to the balanced state of gratitude and love. I truly believe that our external eco-system (social circle), our intuition and our body are giving us feedback to awaken us to the ever presence of love. Our body is basically a love and gratitude-seeking organism. It wants us to feel appreciation and love.

The body never lies.
– MARTHA GRAHAM

I have seen many patients and seminar attendees who have experienced amazing transformational "healings" because they awakened themselves gratefully to the ever-present power of love. I once consulted with a gentleman in San Francisco who had psoriasis. He had difficulty acknowledging outwardly his inner love for his father and was anxious thinking he could never live up to his expectations. He dissolved these emotions using the Demartini Method®, and his skin started healing the next day, and within several weeks it was completely clear. I have seen partial baldness transform and hair grow back when people opened their heart with the power of the Gratitude Effect. I have seen colds and flu symptoms clear up, and I have seen jaw tightness and TJM stress disappear. I have seen immune systems return to normal when people clear themselves of major anger or resentment.

It all starts with gratitude. That's when our physical body is functioning at its maximum capacity. If we see disorder on the outside, we create disorder on the inside. Whether we have a back pain because we feel we have "lost" something, or whether it's our shoulders letting us know that we feel burdened, whatever it is, it's just an indicator that we have some unbalanced perceptions. The moment we gratefully balance them, our body responds. The moment our minds are truly grateful, our physiology starts to change.

Your task is not to seek love, but merely to seek and find all the barriers within yourself that you have built against it.

– JALAL AD-DIN RUMI

Your intuition is prompting you to discover the challenges concerning sharing and receiving love and appreciation. Just a couple of days ago, I received an email from a young man who had broken up with his girlfriend and had developed a major illness. He was able to change his perspective on his condition though, and he is healing now. Here is a portion of his letter he wrote to me from the hospital "I've been recently given a challenge in my life, and I've been ill for the past two months. I went to see four practitioners and was sent to the hospital. I'm seeking love with this illness. I'm using this as a way to push myself to grow and to do things I wanted to do for years. Benefits of this illness are great indeed."

We get frightened and we run our immune system down. Stress occurs when we stretch or shrink the truth. When we lie, we experience tensions and compressions in our body, but the Gratitude Effect takes away stress and disorder. It opens our hearts to the truth that everything is love – as it is.

I have seen patterns where people have all their major injuries on the right side, and they have a problem with their father, for example. Some people have all their issues on the left side: either their heart valve is not functioning properly, or their left leg is broken, or they've broken their collarbone or their shoulder on the left side. Some people believe that there are correlations between mother and father issues, and I've certainly seen some patterns where people would swear, "I never want to be like my father" and end up with all their problems or injuries on their right side. But it doesn't matter to gratitude. It helps heal everything and brings both sides into balance. It makes you more certain because you don't perceive the outer disorder anymore. Your dis-ease dissolves, and you become more present. You are not living in the past or the future with those imbalances – you awaken to the "now" because of the Gratitude Effect.

Emotions Can Kill, but They Don't Have to

Emotion always has its roots in the unconscious and manifests itself in the body.
– *IRENE CLAREMONT DE CASTILLEJO*

The two basic emotions, fear and guilt, are the most alarming to our overall physical and emotional well-being. These two imbalanced perceptions can negatively affect our vitality and physiology and disturb our inner poise. They can literally and gradually cause our bodies to self-destruct by linking them to a number of life-threatening diseases. But what exactly are they?

Fear is nothing but a distorted imagination of the future, which arises when we assume unrealistically that we are about to experience more losses than gains, more drawbacks than benefits, more negative than positive experiences, or more pains than pleasures. It results from an imbalanced "pro-jection" onto the future when we refuse to see the harmony and balance of life in advance.

Guilt is just a distorted memory of the past, which arises when we unrealistically assume that we have caused ourselves or others more losses than gains, more drawbacks than benefits, more negative than positive experiences, or more pains than pleasures. It results from an imbalanced "re-jection" of the past when we are unwilling to see the harmony and balance in retrospect.

Our emotions fluctuate with our mind's perceptions. We can feel like we are victims of personal circumstances and illness when we refuse to acknowledge the perfect balance of things, or we can return to well-being when we truly discover this inherent harmony. It is entirely up to us. When we reawaken to the balance we initiate and experience the Gratitude Effect.

Our physiology responds to fear and guilt immediately. Any unbalanced perceptions lead to unbalanced neurological and hormonal responses. It is these responses that result in distorted cellular energetics, sometimes labeled as illnesses. Imbalanced perceptions are just another name for stress, which can run our immune systems down and leave us vulnerable to many psychosomatic conditions.

Many other emotions like frustration, anger, depression, and apathy are simply degrees of these responses. Unrealistic expectations, delusions or fantasies held in our minds can lead to the initial unbalanced perception. Unless these expectations are brought down into reality, stress, fear and guilt based illnesses can be the result.

The people who say they don't have time to take care of themselves will soon discover they're spending all their time being sick.
– *PATRICIA ALEXANDER*

Some schools of psychology insist that we need to release, express or get out our pent up emotions. They would say that we need to get our anger out and not hold it in. I think this is not ultimately the wisest approach. I think it is wiser to dissolve the source of such imbalanced emotions by realizing what these emotions truly represent, and what they are trying to teach us. Seeing the underlying hidden order in them and coming to the state of gratitude by understanding the lessons that anger is trying to teach us can be quite powerful.

I believe sharing balanced gratitude is more important than sharing lopsided emotions. I don't consider gratitude an emotion. Elation and depression, attraction and repulsion, positive and negative polarities are all emotions. I call EMOTIONS Energy in MOTION. They are half-perceptions. If I see more positives than negatives, or more negatives than positives, then I'm run by my misperception, and I experience emotions. When I see both perceptions at once, I feel gratitude and love.

Gratitude sits in the centre along with love, enthusiasm and inspiration. These are the four cardinal feelings, but I don't call them emotions. Emotions cause us to avoid or seek something. True gratitude is freedom from such polarities. When we are grateful, we open up our heart. Our love is in the heart. When love of the heart comes out, our mind becomes inspired, and our body becomes enthused.

When we become grateful for something, it stops running our life. We are free. There is true gratitude, and there is false one. When we are grateful for things that only support us, it's the incomplete or false kind. The true gratitude occurs when we embrace both the support and the challenge of our values equally. It is the simultaneous acknowledgment of both support and challenge that awakens us to the Gratitude Effect.

Some patients I see are actually drawing into their bodies the diseased thoughts of their minds.

– ZACHARTY BERCOVITZ

By asking ourselves emotionally balancing questions we can awaken to an empowering state of gratitude. Gratitude can dissolve even the most difficult emotions like despair. If we feel despair, it means we don't know what to do or where to go. It means we are comparing our current reality to some unrealistic illusion, and as a result, acknowledging only drawbacks without seeing the benefits. We are stifled. But there is a way out – you guessed it – through gratitude. No matter what is happening in your life, stop and ask yourself, "How is this serving me and helping me reach my true highest objectives?" Keep asking, keep answering, and keep searching for answers until you see the hidden balance and perfection.

The world is perfectly balanced, and the heart only opens when the mind becomes aware of this perfect harmony. Unbalanced emotions close it down. Although there is a place for the many healing modalities and treatments we can seek for health and relaxation, it is essential that we realise that all true wellness starts in the mind and works through the heart.

How I Held a Miracle in My Hands

Surrender is faith that the power of love can accomplish anything... even when you cannot foresee the outcome.

– *DEEPAK CHOPRA*

Let me share an incredible story of a healing. Soon after I opened my first practice, I was referred a patient whom I will never forget, and, after reading his story, neither will you. When he was thirteen years old, he was playing on top of the stairs in his apartment complex in Mexico, and one of his friends pushed him. He fell down the stairs and broke open his skull. He had been in coma since that time. When his parents brought him into my office, he was sixteen.

His parents spoke limited English, but I learnt that they had taken him to countless hospitals in Mexico and in Texas, and the verdict was always the same – incurable – brain damaged encephalitis with decerebrate rigidity. No doctor would accept him as a patient. They had nowhere else to go. At the time I was known among Houston healing community as "a daring guy" because I would take on cases no one else would. That's how such patients were referred to me.

On the day of the initial consultation, I saw this young teenager's parents walking down the hallway towards my exam room past my office and carrying something wrapped in a white sheet. I wasn't sure what it was. I didn't know what to expect, but I can tell you right now, I wasn't ready for what I saw. His body was so rigid (due to the decerebrate rigidity) that his fingers, hands and toes were curled up. He had a tube passing down through his nose and into his stomach, and he was extremely malnutritioned as his family had been feeding him beans and rice. He had a diaper on, and they had been using suppositories to clean his system out. Being sixteen years old, he weighed less than sixty pounds. Part of his chin was ulcerated as a result of his wrists and fists digging into it, and some of his hair were missing. His eyes were motionless.

I didn't know exactly how to proceed and was literally shaking as I could see that this was not a simple case. I did the best I could to examine him and did an x-ray of his whole spine, which drew my attention to the fact that his skull was jammed onto the spinal cord. I thought maybe after falling down the stairs, he had landed on it and had completely compressed it. I did not sleep at all that night. I wondered what would happen if I lifted his skull from his remaining spine. That was all I could think about that night.

Synchronously, the next morning most of my other patients mysteriously cancelled, so I was free to focus completely on my coma patient. The boy was lying on the table and I was getting ready to adjust him. I was surrounded by people who were waiting anxiously to see what was going to happen. There were four interns, another doctor, my assistant, the boy's mother and father, and seven of his siblings. I was haunted by the vision of his skull jammed on the spinal cord. And lifting it was the only thing I could see in my mind to help this young teenager. Before I did anything, I looked up at the mother and father and said,

"I do not know if I can help your son, but I found something that I feel would be wise to do – to adjust his skull and lift it off the spine."

His mother looked at me, and what she said changed my life. She said,

"Dr. Demartini. If he lives, we rejoice. If he dies, we accept. But we have nowhere else to go. Please help us."

I learnt about the power of unconditional love all over again. With her words, she gave me permission to allow her son to live or die in my hands. I had to be willing to take that risk. So I did. I entered some kind of trance state and became very present, and then I lifted his skull off his spine with a force like I had not ever experienced – I felt as if the universe was working through me. All of a sudden his fingers uncurled, his hands opened up, he raised his head, and his eyes opened. He began shrieking and crying like a newborn child. His whole body started moving all over the table.

In a split second his entire family went on their hands and knees, praying. I needed a moment to take it all in. I walked into the adjacent office, and the other doctor followed me in there, we sat at a table across from each other, grabbed hands and began to cry. We both witnessed a chiropractic adjustment the like of which we had never seen before – it felt miraculous. We saw the power that brought life to a lifeless body. We saw that when a spine is out of alignment, it can block the expression of the power of life animating the body, the spirit, the brain, the nervous system.

I started working with that boy every day. In a matter of months, he gained twenty pounds. He didn't need the tube in his nose anymore because he was learning to chew and swallow food. He didn't need suppositories anymore either. He gained awareness and his eyes regained movement. Then one day, just as I was finishing his adjustment, he slowly and unexpectedly turned his face toward the end of the table where his mother and father were holding his feet; his mouth began to move and quiver, and his innermost yearning to communicate again manifested through the words "mama" and "papa". For the first time in three and half years he consciously spoke to his parents.

I learnt a lot about unconditional love and gratitude from this case. I learnt a lot about walking through fear. I was somehow blessed to be there when no one else would help him. I was gifted by the opportunity because no one else would try. I watched limited belief systems being taken over by a vision of possibility. Every day my office team would say an acknowledging prayer of thanks before working with this special teenager, because we all felt extremely grateful to have him. Every chiropractor has patients who are gifts. This teenager was one of my gifts. He further awakened in my mind and heart the Gratitude Effect.

Unleash the Healer Within

The cure for all ills and wrongs, the cares, the sorrows and the crimes of humanity, all lie in the one word 'love.' It is the divine vitality that everywhere produces and restores life.

– LYDIA MARIA CHILD

Within our own minds and hearts, we have the power to heal. Just as unbalanced emotions can lead us into illness, love and appreciation can lead us back to wellness.

The Gratitude Effect has the power to change your life and the lives of those you come in contact with. It is the key to healing, growth and fulfillment. A therapist who works from a space of love and gratitude of the heart, and certainty and presence of the mind will bring healing to anyone he/she comes in contact with. In fact, anyone in the healing arts who applies these four cardinal pillars of healing will become a master healer, just as anyone seeking healing, who applies these four principles, will heal.

There is no greater healer on this planet than the feeling of love. Love is the result of a heart that is open through gratitude and not distorted by the emotions created by lopsided perceptions.

Years ago I was the president of the Cancer Prevention and Control Association in Houston, Texas. At that time I lectured on what I believed to be some of the causes of cancer. Most of the ideas I explored have now become almost mainstream, but at the time they were considered progressive and unorthodox. At the time, a doctor by the name of Carl Simington advocated a technique where you visualized the leukocytes attacking and destroying the cancer cells, and wrote about its effect in helping cancer. That was a major jump forward in terms of understanding the mind's power over the body. Today, however, it is wiser for patients to visualize their body as whole and vital, and to be grateful for how their cancer has awakened their life to the higher importance of love and has brought their attention to the issues in their life they haven't loved."

Carl came to the realization that everything serves the purpose of teaching love. I define illness as the illusions of health and disease, and wellness as the synthesis. Since disease may just simply be healing turned inside out. Anything we see that is not loved represents a distortion in our perceptions and is ultimately our lie. It creates uncertainties and our desire to fix and change things – it's a dissipation of energy that is called disease. Every emotion we have has its corresponding manifestation in the body that is trying to wake us up to the imbalanced lie that we're living.

The second pillar is gratitude, an absolute appreciation for the balance of life – as it is. If we're not appreciative, we don't easily grow – appreciation is an absolutely essential component of the growth and maintenance of a body. In fact your body will give you symptoms and create illness to try to get you to appreciate it and your life.

All of us are on what some have termed spiritual missions. We are here for the purpose of learning lessons of gratitude and love. Everything we do in all the seven areas of life will be teaching us exactly that, and to the degree we learn those lessons, we will unfold our full potential physically and mentally. When we are grateful for life, we open up the gateway of the heart and allow the love that is always waiting there to eternally express itself in the form of light or illumination in our consciousness. This light brings organization and order to human physiology. It's been shown scientifically that love and appreciation organize and bring order to cell structures on a molecular level.

Certainty, the third pillar, is a by-product of gratitude and love. When you are certain, you're not wavering with past remembered guilt and future imagined fears – the emotions. Instead, you're present, and hence, the fourth pillar is presence. Love, gratitude, certainty, and presence – those are the four cardinal pillars that support the dome of healing, and any healer who has those states can bring healing to anyone. And guess what? We all have the potential to be a healer, so unleash the healer within by awakening the Gratitude Effect.

Questions to Help You See the Perfect Balance

- How is (has) my "disease" serving (served) me in all seven areas of life?
- What are its underlying benefits that I can be grateful for?
- How does (did) it help my life mission?
- How is (has) it ultimately helping (helped) me be whole and well?

Go back to every illness, injury or accident you have experienced and have never been able to say thank you for and ask the above questions.

Affirmations to Help You Appreciate Your Body and Heal

- My body is a love-seeking organism that's guiding me to make sure I truly love.
- I am thankful for my body because it gives me instant feedback. Before I consciously know, it already knows. It doesn't lie to me. It's letting me know what I am truly thinking.
- I am grateful for my hair.
- I am grateful for my skin.
- I am grateful for my heartbeat.
- I am grateful for my breath.
- I am grateful for my body's amazing healing ability.
- I am grateful that my body works. I am grateful for billions and trillions of cells. that are functioning everyday. I am grateful for the intelligence that is running it.
- My love is the greatest of all my healers.
- I love how I look, I look incredible.
- I love how I feel, I feel grateful and loved.
- I am true to myself, I simply shine.
- My body is such an inspiration to work with.
- I am inspired and my deep breathing shows it.
- I use my body wisely.
- I sleep soundly.
- I keep my body clean inside and out.
- I eat wholesome foods that maximize my life.
- I eat exactly the right amount of food to remain toned, slim and youthful.
- My energy is infinite for I recognize its source.

- I am flexible in body, mind and soul.
- My body is a temple that radiates light and love.
- I love being surrounded by the healing miracles of nature.
- I feel young even as I am supposedly getting older.
- Every cell of my body is vibrating with love.
- My vitality, stamina and tone are phenomenal.
- I have endurance and I am vibrant.
- I am moderate, rhythmic and consistent.
- I have organized my life so beautifully.

Exercises to Reintroduce You to Your Own Magnificence

Exercise 1. Think about your head. How can you be grateful for it? How does it serve you? Your hair? Your scalp? Your eyes? Skin, nose, lips? In your mind, go through your body from head to toe and think how you can be grateful for each and every part inside and outside of you. Recognize the magnificence of your body and find a way to look at it in a new way – with awe and gratitude.

Exercise 2. Be aware of your body – do not just expect it to maintain its own wellbeing without any contribution or effort on your part. Think of your body as a gift you have been given that is serving to enrich the entire structure and fulfillment of your life. Tend your body and take care of it – as you would tend or take care of garden.

CHAPTER 9

Final Thoughts on Gratitude

What I Was Grateful for When I Had Nothing

If we had no winter, the spring would not be so pleasant;
if we did not sometimes have a taste of adversity,
prosperity would not be so welcome.
– *ANNE DUDLEY BRADSTREET*

Many people look at my current lifestyle and say, "Sure, it's easy to be grateful when you travel around the world doing what you love without having to worry about money." That's true. I have a wonderful life now. But even when I lived on the streets and had nothing, or slept hiding behind the garbage containers to keep safe or on top of steam vents to keep warm, I was able to find many things to be grateful for.

One thing that I was especially grateful for was diners because on more than one occasion they kept me from going without food. One time, on my way hitchhiking to California, I got dropped off at a truck stop. The driver was going to sleep in his truck, so he asked me to get out. I thanked him for the ride and went over to the diner. It's open all night. You can sit in there, but you can't sleep or lean your head on the table. You have to sleep outside.

When I went inside the diner, I walked around to check out where there was food left over on plates. I sat down and ate whatever food I found, like pieces of bread or sausage, or tomatoes. Anything that was edible I would eat. I tried to do it discreetly so they wouldn't kick me out. I moved from table to table a couple of times, and finally this lady behind the counter saw me and called me.

I thought, "Oh, no, she's going to kick me out." But she said, "Come here and sit down. What do you want? It's on the house. I am buying it." She fed me as a mother would. She paid around two dollars for my meal. In those days that amount was a lot. The price of toast was roughly twenty cents. I was grateful for that meal and thanked her. Somehow, I was always taken care of. And right after I ate, I found something else to be grateful for – I got a ride. A guy asked,

"Hey, where are you going, kid?"

I said, "I'm going to California."

"Well, I'm going to Blythe, and if that will get you part of the way there, I'll give you a ride."

"Great. I'd sure appreciate that. Do you mind if I rest in your car because I haven't slept all night?"

"No problem. I'll be up till the sunrise. I'll tell you when we get to Blythe."

I thanked him and went to sleep, grateful for the ride. We got to Blythe, and I found another ride. A guy asked me if I had any money to pay for the ride, and I said that I had thirteen bucks.

He said, "Well, you have more than I thought you did, but not enough for me to take it from you. If you help me fix my car, I'll give you a ride to Idyllwild."

I said, "Fabulous. I appreciate that."

I knew enough about cars to be able to change a tire. So I helped him fix his car, got all greasy and dirty, but I got a ride. He was thankful for me, and I was thankful for him.

He asked me a few hours later, "Are you hungry?"

I said, "Yeah."

"Let's get some dates."

He bought a bag of dates for two dollars, and I ate sweet dates all the way to Idyllwild, where I got off. Idyllwild was then not a large city. It was a beautiful mountain town, but when I got off there, I was in the middle of nowhere. I couldn't get a ride because it was off the freeway. I didn't know to get off sooner when we were still on the freeway, so I had to walk through the town looking for a ride. Eventually, I found a ride back to the freeway, and I was on the road again.

I was grateful for the rides and for anything else along the way. I guess my mom taught me to be grateful, so it was natural for me to find things to be grateful for. When I had close calls with death, I would be grateful simply to be alive. It's all a matter of perspective. Every event in your life is attempting to awaken within you the Gratitude Effect.

The Hardest Things to be Grateful for

The only real mistake is the one from which we learn nothing.
–*JOHN POWELL*

From my experience of working with tens of thousands of people over all these years, I found that for many of them the hardest things to be grateful for were their own so-called "mistakes" and the so-called "loss" of their loved ones. I would like to share some thoughts on these two ghosts that haunt many hearts, thus preventing them from the inspiring experience of all encompassing love and gratitude.

Sometime you may imagine that it is necessary to forgive someone, since you think that they may have made a mistake. But in actuality there are no mistakes. We only perceive certain actions to be mistakes when we have not looked deep enough and realized that at any one moment others are only acting according to their values, not necessarily our own. We also imagine at times that it is necessary to forgive ourselves for the things we've done. Again this is because we have not probed deep enough into the action to see a hidden and balanced order. There is nothing ultimately to forgive, only something to discover a greater order in. Mistakes are ultimately based on perceptual illusions. If you think you made a mistake, you may be thinking too much of yourself and assuming that you can disturb the hidden balance in the universe. I assure you that whatever you have done or not done has served someone in some way.

Recently one fine young man told me he was sorry that he was mean to his mother.

I asked him, "When you were challenging her, who was nice and supportive of her at the same time?"

"No one"

"Look again."

"Okay, my sister."

"Did your mother and sister have some differences, and did they get closer at that moment because you were mean to her?"

"Yes, they did."

"By becoming mean, did you also become more independent from her?"

"Yes."

"Is that what your mother wanted for you – to stand

independently on your own two feet?"

"Yes, I think I see."

"Let me ask you, when you rejected her, who did you get closer to?"

"My girlfriend."

"Who has become a new mother figure for you? Nothing is ever missing – it only changes form."

"Her mother and I got close."

"Do you see the balance of love in that situation? So where is the mistake?"

"I don't see one any more."

"There never was."

The only so-called "mistake" is not seeing the hidden balance and order in life. Things that we label extremely positive can become addicting to us and become objects of infatuation. If we perceive ourselves losing them, we feel loss. If things that we dislike leave our life, we celebrate. We don't ever have the feeling of loss over the things we resent. Only losing the things we are infatuated with causes the withdrawal symptoms of grief, remorse, bereavement, sorrow, and so forth.

Fearing the loss of something is not a sign of love, but a sign of addiction. Your withdrawal symptoms are letting you know that you haven't loved it yet, and it is still running your life. A broken heart is actually setting you free. You don't have to be addicted to someone else and minimize yourself in relation to him/her. You can be the authentic you again. When you love someone or something, you are not afraid to lose it. Whether it comes or goes, you still love it and you feel its presence in your heart.

Another sign of wisdom is to see that the moment something disappears from your life, it appears in a different form that you recognize. For example, you may get a new boyfriend, and three of your best friends disappear from your life. He breaks up with you, and at that moment your friends appear again to bring love and attention into your life. There's never a gain or a loss. There is just a transformation. And if you can immediately see it, you have just begun mastering your life. Stress is the inability to adapt to an ever-changing environment. The Gratitude Effect expresses pure adaptability.

I recently worked with a lady whose husband had passed away a month before. She was grieving and feeling the loss.

I asked her, "What are you missing the most?"

"I miss him."

I said, "Surely, you don't miss all of him. I bet you don't miss his dirty clothes on the floor, and you don't miss his hair in the sink, and you don't miss his angry or sloppy side."

She said, "Well, that's true."

"So, you only miss parts of him. What are they?"

"Well, I miss his confidence."

"Okay. The moment he passed away, who has shown up in your life with this form of confidence? It could be one person or many."

She said, "Yes, my brother came back into my life, and my father showed a lot of confidence too. Husbands of my two friends were very confident in helping me deal with this loss. My son has suddenly grown up and gained more confidence than ever."

"Can you see that confidence has emerged in your life in other forms through different people?"

"Yes, I can see that now."

Then I asked her, "What was the drawback of your recent husband's confidence?"

She needed a moment to think, "Well, I guess he could be rude because he thought he knew everything. Sometimes he could be frustrated and impatient with me because I would be slow in getting things."

I had to break her addiction to her fantasy by pointing out the equal number of drawbacks in his confidence, so that it didn't have more positives than negatives anymore. Now it was just neutral. I also pointed to the new form of confidence in her life and asked her about its benefits.

She said, "I just love seeing my son more confident. He had never seemed to demonstrate that before." I helped her see that her husband's confidence had both benefits and drawbacks, and that the new forms of it were there, and they were just as great. After this, I asked her, "So, do you miss his confidence?"

She said, "I don't feel like I miss it any more."

"What else do you miss?"

We had to utilize the Demartini Method®, and with a series of questions, we balanced her mind and broke her infatuations, addictions, and illusions so that she could have an appreciation of both the old and the new forms. We sat down for about thirty minutes, and we went through five things that she thought she had lost, and after we were done, I asked her, "Are you missing anything about him now?"

And she said, "No. I feel that in a way he is surrounding me. It's like he is present in all my friends and my son."

I said, "You are right, he is present. Honour his presence. When you die, do you want people who love you to feel remorse?"

"No. I want them to go on with their lives."

"Why would you feel remorse for him then? That's not honouring him. He would want you to live your life to the fullest."

She said, "That's exactly what he wanted when we had talked about it."

"Appreciate his presence in different forms, and break your addiction to one bodily form. We get addicted to the form, and then we feel loss."

We cleared it, and her remorse was gone. The Gratitude Effect transformed her grief into understanding and love.

There is Nothing but Love

Behind it all is surely an idea so simple, so beautiful, so compelling that when – in a decade, a century, a millennium – we grasp it, we will say to each other, how could it have been otherwise? How can we have been so blind for so long?

– *JOHN WHEELER*

As a species, human beings have developed and evolved with the help of both support and challenge, kindness and cruelty, peace and war. We are surrounded by growth and decay, building and destruction, life and death, union and division. It is our destiny to live with this magnificent balance in order to be whole. Though we may be lifted by the colourful beauty of spring flowers before us, distantly we are synchronously brought down by the colourless ugliness of the fallen leaves. Our emotions go through cycles of hot and cold just like Earth goes through the four seasons. We sing of joy and scream of sorrow; we like and admire, as well as dislike and despise. We come close and go away; we join and separate. We boast our inner calm and withdraw to our inner turmoil. Peace treaties are hailed, as war declarations emerge loathed.

Though we often seek one without its opposite, the pairs of opposites are inseparable. It is the whole we are destined for, not just a part. And we don't have to get rid of half of our nature to love our true selves. Clear and misty, sunny and cloudy all serve the purpose of our growth and evolution. Foolishly we seek one side of life's coin only to be awakened from our slumber by its opposite; for both are teachers of our soul.

Nowhere in nature do such one-sided follies exist but in our minds. As one emerges, so does its opposite – they always walk hand in hand. When will we abandon our foolishness and wake up to nature's balancing ways? When will we acknowledge the universal harmony of opposites? My enemy is my friend, and my friend is my enemy. Support me and I will depend; challenge me and you will set me free. Why can't we see the harmony of the two as one and the necessity of them both to soften and strengthen us along our journey on the path of divine order and grace? Love is but a dance of such opposites. We need both to live and grow. From this deeper understanding comes the Gratitude Effect.

The Secret Wisdom of Your Inner Voice

Words are the voice of the heart
– *CONFUCIUS*

You can acquire the deeper understanding of the Gratitude Effect, build great wisdom and discover your genius by spending time each day in grateful communion with your inner voice. What better way of creating a more fulfilling life than by mastering the art of tuning into your most inspired and ingenious self, your inner voice! This voice is your guide of all guides to a life of greatness. You cannot attune to this inspiring voice without living a more inspiring life. Genius, creativity, and a silent power emerge from your heart and mind the moment you do.

The secret of tuning in to its magnificent messages is having a heart filled with gratitude. When your heart is open wide with gratitude, your inner voice becomes loud and clear, and your most life expanding messages enter your mind with ease. If your heart is filled with gratitude, it is almost impossible to stop your inner voice from speaking its wisdom clearly and profoundly.

As your voice on the inside grows in clarity and strength, so will your inspiration when you listen. Begin to attune to that inspiring station from within. Listen as it guides you to new levels of creativity and inspired action. Your inner voice will put few or no limits on your life. Only the many outer voices of mediocrity will do so. Decide now to expand your wisdom and fulfillment through this careful listening.

When you are truly grateful, you will receive amazing and inspiring inner messages. These messages will be more powerful than might at first be apparent. The master, the genius, is the one who listens carefully. These priceless gems of guiding revelation will assist you in living a life of greatness.

Be sure to act on your inspirations as soon as possible. When you don't follow the inspirations and intuitions of your inner voice promptly, you can begin to emotionally build or beat your self up. But it is also part of the grand design of conscious evolution. No matter what happens, you will eventually learn and unfold your inner spiritual mission, talent, and destiny because life events will force you to listen to that wise voice within.

Today, you have an opportunity for expanding your greatness. When your wise and masterful voice on the inside becomes greater than the many little voices on the outside, a life of great fulfillment, wisdom and genius can become yours and the Gratitude Effect takes over.

Watch your thoughts, for they become words.
Watch your words, for they become actions.
Watch your actions, for they become habits.
Watch your habits, for they become character.
Watch your character, for it becomes your destiny.
– *FRANK OUTLAW*

Listening to your inner voice is very important, but so is talking to yourself. Did you know that every word you say leaves an imprint in your mind – particularly when they are aligned harmoniously with your highest values? And did you know that every statement you repeat, whether true or false, whether to yourself or to others, becomes integrated into your conscious and unconscious belief systems? So, what kind of conversations are you having with yourself, and what are you telling yourself?

When you say something to yourself, you don't even have to believe it in order for the brain reactions to start. But once these reactions begin, mind imprints are created, and they lead your mind to believing and living these statements regardless. Repetition is the key to building any new habit, so it is wise to begin including into your daily language those words that will inspire you most to fulfill your dreams.

First, you might want to write down the most inspiring statements you can imagine, ones you would love to say to yourself every day for the rest of your life. When you use clear, definite, and specific statements, they release tremendous internal power from within you that can help you transform your life and help you become attuned to what you intend to do. When I write these powerful messages, I find it helpful to use concise statements in the present tense. I usually use statements that inspire loving feelings and describe realities that are possible. You have seen numerous examples of these at the end of each chapter.

If you begin saying these inspiring statements to yourself inwardly or outwardly at least three times daily, soon you will see a shift in your belief system. Declare them emphatically with feeling and with certainty as if they were already true and presently being lived.

You might also want to record these powerful statements on any portable audio device in your own voice or ask someone else who inspires you to record them for you, so you can listen to them as often as possible. Consider having your favourite piece of music playing in the background while you prepare this recording.

What you say to yourself does make a difference. Your daily conversations with yourself can make you or break you. Words have the power to remould your destiny. Begin today to shift your life in the direction of your choice with great and inspiring words of power. Declare to yourself whatever will awaken from within your heart the Gratitude Effect.

How to Start Your Journey with Gratitude Today

A journey of a thousand miles begins with a single step.
– *CONFUCIUS*

Why not start your journey of gratitude today? The impact of being grateful is powerful in all seven areas of life. Gratitude elevates our state of being, enlightens our awareness and inspires our greatest actions. On the other hand, ingratitude weighs you down and brings you down. Our immune system runs down, our spiritual life feels like hell, our mind becomes clouded when we are ungrateful. When we are in such a state, who will want to do business with us? Our financial situation is more likely to become stagnant and devalued. We will probably become more isolated from people because others wouldn't want to stay with someone who doesn't appreciate them.

True gratitude gives us a moment of fulfillment and love for life, for our existence, and for what is, as it is right now. Gratitude is the number one tool to make us grow. The Gratitude Effect is the expansion effect for every human being on the planet. Nelson Mandela once said that we serve the world by shining, not shrinking.

I once had a great teacher who said, "If there is a day in your life that you cannot be grateful for, it's wise to go back and look at that day from a different perspective, with different eyes until you see its purpose with a feeling of gratitude. Otherwise, you will carry that day into tomorrow. You will never be able to be fully present tomorrow because you will still be stuck in that day." I followed his advice and found it so beneficial that I want to invite you to do the same. Go back to the earliest memories of your life, and take every single memory that you haven't been grateful for and ask, "How did it serve me and others?"

Ask this question over and over until you become grateful for the event. Once you are up to date, make it a daily routine. Anything you can't be grateful for becomes baggage. The more ingratitude people accumulate in their life, the more they are stuck in the past, and that, in turn, creates fears of the future and guilt of the past, and prevents them from being inspired and present.

Go back through your life and write thank you notes to everyone involved, and that includes you. Try doing it every morning and every night. Start a gratitude journal. I started one for you at the end of this book. Research has proven that people who keep gratitude journals accomplish more, feel more, and heal more. They are overall more fulfilled. So, reap the benefits of being grateful and make your life amazing through continuously applying the Gratitude Effect.

To Realize

At the touch of love everyone becomes a poet.

– PLATO

I want to finish with words of wisdom that caught my attention as I was browsing the Internet. The origin of this letter is unknown, but its wisdom is touching hearts around the globe. Hope you enjoy it too.

To realize the value of one year – ask a student who has failed a final exam.

To realize the value of nine months – ask a mother who gave birth to a stillborn.

To realize the value of one month – ask a mother who has given birth to a premature baby.

To realize the value of one week – ask an editor of a weekly newspaper.

To realize the value of one hour – ask the lovers who are waiting to meet.

To realize the value of one minute – ask a person who has missed the train, bus or aeroplane.

To realize the value of one second – ask a person who has survived an injury.

To realize the value of one millisecond – ask the person who has won a silver medal in the Olympics.

To realize the value of a loved one – have them leave.

Time waits for no one.

Treasure every moment you have.

Thank You!

Thank you for joining me on this journey of gratitude.
May the profound power lying within you now become revealed.
May your heart of love and mind of wisdom guide your actions to your highest fulfillment.
May you become awakened to the power of your hidden inner balance and harmony.
May you do what you love and love what you do.
May your inner gifts inspire your outer powers.
May the clarity of your vision unleash unlimited vitality.
You are a genius and you apply your wisdom.

Gratitude Journal

In my daily gratitude journal, I start each statement of appreciation with these or similar words: "Today I had the opportunity to..." You might want to begin each statement in your journal this way, create your own format, or use no format at all. The format is not what is most important. What is most important is to develop the daily habit of being grateful for the many events filling your life. I challenge you to try this habit for one month and not miss a day. I am certain that you will experience a major shift in your thinking, feeling and actions and you will be amazed at how dramatically the Gratitude Effect can inspire and transform your life.

Day 1.

Day 2.

Day 3.

Day 4.

Day 5.

Day 6.

Day 7.

Day 8.

Day 9.

Day 10.

Day 11.

Day 12.

Day 13.

Day 14.

Day 15.

Day 16.

Day 17.

Day 18.

Day 19.

Day 20.

Day 21.

Day 22.

Day 23.

Day 24.

Day 25.

Day 26.

Day 27.

Day 28.

Day 29.

Day 30.

Day 31.

About the Author

Dr John F. Demartini is an international speaker and consultant who breathes life and enthusiasm into his audiences with his enlightening perspectives, humorous observations of human nature and practical action steps. When he speaks, hearts open, minds become inspired and people are motivated into action. His gentle, fun, and informative teachings mingle entertaining stories with trans-formational wisdom and insights. His trail-blazing philosophy and revolutionary understanding is reshaping modern psychology and business and transforming the lives of millions. As a retired chiropractor, researcher, writer and philosopher, his studies have made him a leading expert on healing, human potential and philosophy.

Dr Demartini is the founder of the *Demartini Human Research and Education Foundation.* He is also the creator of *The Breakthrough Experience®* seminar and originator of *The Demartini Method®*. He has written several dozens of books, including best-selling books entitled *Count Your Blessings - The Healing Power of Gratitude and Love; The Breakthrough Experience® - A Revolutionary New Approach to Personal Transformation; How to Make One Hell of a Profit and Still Get to Heaven, You Can Have an Amazing Life in Just 60 Days, Beyond Blame – Flowers to Plant in the Garden of Your Mind, The Heart of Love – How to Go Beyond Fantasy to True Relationship Fulfillment* and *The Riches Within – Your Seven Secret Treasures.*

Articles and feature stories about Dr Demartini and his insightful personal and professional development methodologies have appeared in numerous international magazines and newspapers. He has appeared on hundreds of radio and television news and talk shows and several film documentaries. As a presenter, Dr Demartini has shared his transformative principles and methodologies in conferences to business executives, health professionals, financial managers and consultants working in the field of human consciousness and has presented along side many other well respected speaking professionals including Rupert Sheldrake, William Tiller, Peter Russell, Wayne Dyer, Deepak Chopra, Donald Beck, Fritjof Capra, Nathaniel Brandon, Andrew Weil, Gary Schwartz, Stephen Covey and many more. As a pioneer on the frontier of human consciousness and an explorer of the ultimate nature of reality, Dr Demartini is also a leader in the field of psycho-spiritual development & transformation.

Dr Demartini also is a private consultant, advising people from all walks of life on personal and professional development and achievement. These include Wall Street financiers, corporate executives, health professionals, politicians, Hollywood stars and sports personalities... His many clients use his expertise and wisdom to assist in keeping their lives, health, relationships, attitudes and business acumen steadily on track.

For more information
Call: 888-DEMARTINI or 713-850-1234
or Fax: 713-850-9239
www.drdemartini.com
info@drdemartini.com